POLAND
LAND OF FREEDOM FIGHTERS

By Christine Pfeiffer

ᗡP DILLON PRESS, INC.
Minneapolis, Minnesota 55415

Photographic Acknowledgments

The photographs have been reproduced through the courtesy of: Anna Beata Bohadziewicz; Cameramann International; Congressman Daniel Rostenkowski; Consulate General of Poland in Chicago; Embassy of the Republic of Poland; Christine Pfeiffer; Polaska Agencja Interpress Fotoservis; Polish National Tourist Bureau.

Library of Congress Cataloging-in-Publication Data

Pfeiffer, Christine.
   Poland, land of freedom fighters / by Christine Pfeiffer.
     p. cm.—(Discovering our heritage)
   Includes bibliographical references and index.
   Summary: Discusses the people, traditions, folkways, holidays, family life, food, schools, sports, recreations, and history of Poland
    ISBN 0-87518-464-2
    1. Poland—Juvenile literature. [1. Poland.] I. Title.
II. Series.
DK4147.P46 1991
943.8—dc20   90-26093
                                             CIP
                                             AC

Dillon Press, Inc., 242 Portland Avenue South
Minneapolis, Minnesota 55415
Printed in the United States of America

1 2 3 4 5 6 7 8 9 99 98 97 96 95 94 93 92 91

Contents

Fast Facts about Poland

Official Name: Polska Rzeczypolita (Republic of Poland)

Capital: Warsaw

Location: Poland is a large central European nation that
borders the Soviet Union to the east, Czechoslovakia
to the south, Germany to the west, and the Baltic Sea
to the north

Area: 120,725 square miles (312,677 square kilometers);
Greatest Distances: north-south—395 miles (636
kilometers); east-west—430 miles (692 kilometers);
Coastline: 277 miles (446 kilometers)

Elevation: *Highest*—Rysy Peak, 8,199 feet (2,499 me-
ters) above sea level; *Lowest*—sea level

Population: *Estimated 1989 Population*—38,200,000;
Distribution—61 percent live in or near cities; 39
percent live in rural areas; *Density*—313 persons per
square mile (121 per square kilometer)

Form of Government: Parliamentary Republic

Important Products: *Agriculture*—barley, hogs, rye,
sugar beets, wheat, potatoes; *Manufacturing*—iron,
chemicals, food products, steel, machinery, ships

Basic Unit of Money: zloty

Major Language: Polish

Major Religions: A large majority of Poles are Roman

Catholic; Protestants and Jews form small minorities

Flag: Two broad, horizontal stripes—white on top and red on bottom—form the national flag flown by the people; a state flag, sometimes flown by the government, features an eagle in a coat of arms in the middle of the white stripe; some versions of this flag feature a crowned eagle

National Anthem: "Jeszce Polska nie Zginela" ("Poland Has Not Yet Perished")

Major Holidays: Easter Day; Labor Day—May 1; Saint John's Eve—June 23; Assumption Day—August 15; Saint Nicholas Day—December 6; Christmas Day—December 25

1. Proud to be Polish

"Although for many long years efforts were made to cut Poland off from her ideals, Poland held her ground and is now reaching for the freedom to which she is justly entitled. Together with Poland, other nations of Eastern Europe are following this path. The wall that was separating people from freedom has collapsed. And I hope that the nations of the world will never let it be rebuilt."

In November 1989, a year before he was elected president of Poland, Lech Walesa, longtime leader of Poland's Solidarity trade union and political movement, addressed the United States Congress. He closed his speech with these words. For nearly ten years, Solidarity had worked to give Polish citizens control of their government and economy. It had tried to increase Poland's independence from its huge and powerful neighbor, the Soviet Union (U.S.S.R.).

In the 1980s, Poland's independent values inspired people throughout the world. Eventually, these ideas provided an example for dramatic changes throughout Eastern Europe. Poland was the first East European nation to have an independent trade union. It was also the first since World War II to hold elections in which parties

After nine years of being outlawed, Solidarity holds its Second Congress in April, 1990. Leader Lech Walesa is greeted by Prime Minister Tadeusz Mazowiecki.

that were not Communist had an equal chance of winning.

Suddenly, in 1989, all of Eastern Europe was following Poland's lead. Eastern European nations, and even the Soviet Union itself, were holding negotiations, having multi-party elections, and reducing the role of Communist parties in their governments. They also began to experiment with market-based economies that would be more like those of Western Europe and North America. In a market-based economy, the government does not set prices and determine jobs. Instead, prices, goods, and jobs are controlled by the supply and demand of consumers. Poland's new economic plan is the most dramatic of any nation in the region, and greatly reduces the amount of government control.

Throughout their history, Poles have struggled for their freedom. Their country has once again started to move toward freedom and economic independence. But the recent changes have not ended the challenges facing Poland. There are still many political and economic adjustments and improvements that Poles have to make. Still, despite the problems that the rapid changes have created, Poles are excited for the future of their nation.

Rivers and Boundaries

The present boundaries of Poland and its neighbors were established in 1945, at the end of World War II. Much of Poland's northern border is formed by the coast of the Baltic Sea, and several important port cities are located there. Part of Poland's eastern boundary with the Soviet Union is formed by the Bug River. Near Warsaw, the Polish capital, the Bug branches off from the Vistula, Poland's main river. The Vistula flows for 662 miles (1,059 kilometers) throughout central Poland, making a long, winding line that begins near the southern border and ends at the Baltic Sea. Two other rivers, the Oder and the Neisse, form Poland's western boundary with Germany. Part of the Oder branches off to flow southeast through several Polish cities and into Czechoslovakia, Poland's southern neighbor.

After World War II, Russia solidified its control of the countries east of Poland into the Union of Soviet Socialist Republics. The U.S.S.R. lies east of Poland, but the nearest ethnic people are not Russians, but Lithuanians, Byelorussians, and Ukrainians. For many years, these peoples' lands have been "states," or part, of the U.S.S.R. In 1990, however, Lithuania declared its independence from the Soviet Union. Soon afterward, Estonia and Latvia—which like Lithuania had been independent before World War II—also sought independence. Other republics that have been part of the U.S.S.R. for longer periods, such as the Ukraine and Georgia, have independence movements also. It is not yet clear, though, whether they will leave the Soviet Union. In any case, Poland's neighbors' relationship with the U.S.S.R. may soon change, just as Poland's has.

Government Changes

From 1948 to 1989, one political party, the Polish United Workers' Party, was in charge of running the government. This was a Communist party, so the government owned large businesses and controlled foreign trade. It also set prices, and decided how much each industry should produce. The government also had more control over

mass communications, such as television and radio, than the United States or Canadian governments do.

Since 1989, however, other parties have been allowed to gain power. The current government is run by a coalition, or group of parties. This means that cabinet ministers and other high officials who are members of different political parties run the government together. The head of the Polish United Workers' Party for many years, Wojciech Jaruzelski, was president during the first few years of rapid change. But the first new prime minister, Tadeusz Mazowiecki, is an important member of Solidarity, as is Lech Walesa, who was elected president in December, 1990.

The Polish Peasant Party, the Democratic Party, and other groups also contribute candidates for the Parliament, or *Sejm*. The Sejm meets in Warsaw to pass laws and

From top to bottom: General Wojciech Jaruzelski, ex-Prime Minister Tadeusz Mazowiecki, and current President Lech Walesa.

approve government appointments. Even during the Communist-controlled years, Poles had some choice in their parliamentary representatives. Today, though, those choices have increased. The non-Communist parties have become stronger. Additionally, the Sejm now has two chambers instead of one, so voters have even more representatives.

New Trading Partners

Like other Eastern European countries, Poland is a member of the Warsaw Pact, the military alliance controlled by the Soviets. In a military alliance, countries agree to defend each other in case of war. The Warsaw Pact nations also have many trade agreements. These alliances have historically made Poland's relationship with the Soviet Union a close one, even though Poles have not always agreed with Soviet policies.

However, in November of 1990, the Warsaw Pact and NATO, the alliance that includes Western Europe and the United States, officially declared an end to their rivalry. As a result, they will probably become less important as relations between East and West become closer.

Trade with Western nations has already increased because of the changes in Poland's government. In 1989, Poland made agreements with the United States and the

Many Polish farmers still use traditional equipment.

European Community (the largest group of Western European nations) to increase trade and gain more aid for industry and agriculture.

Farmland

Most of Poland's land is flat and rich, excellent for agriculture. In fact, Poland's name—*Polska* in Polish— comes from the Polish word for field, *pole*. Almost one-third of Poland's 38 million people are farmers. Many of them live in small villages that are hundreds of years old.

Although Polish farmers use modern tractors and scientific farming methods, they also keep many traditional ways. Horses are popular, and a farm family riding along a country road in a horse-drawn wagon is a common sight.

Poland is among the world's top producers of rye, oats, potatoes, and sugar beets. Wheat, milk, and eggs are other important farm products. Poland is also famous for its vodka—a liquor made from grains—and for its fine hams, which are exported all over the world.

Nearly all of Poland's farms are small and privately owned. In most cases, they have been passed down through many generations of a family. There are a few large, government-owned, collective farms like those in the Soviet Union and some other Eastern European countries. But these will probably be divided among private owners as Poland moves towards a market economy. Already, more than 80 percent of Poland's farmland is owned by individuals.

In the past, the government bought most of the crops and set the prices. As the new government becomes stronger, this may no longer be the case.

Growing Industry

Farming is very important in Poland, but so is industry. Polish workers mine coal, manufacture steel—even build and export entire factory production lines! They also make cloth, computers, medicines, and many other products. In the northern port cities of Gdansk, Gdynia, and Szczecin, shipbuilding is an important trade. Lodz, Poland's second largest city, is a textile, metal, and industrial center. Wroclaw is the center of the electronics and computer industries. In the south, thousands of people work in Nowa Huta's gigantic steel mills.

Recent economic problems have hurt the standard of living in Poland. Poles often must wait in long lines to buy many of the things they need, including food. Sometimes certain foods are rationed, meaning that each person or household is allowed to buy a limited amount at one time. During the hard times of the 1980s, millions of Poles waited in line with ration coupons to try to get their share of scarce meat supplies. The new government has not been able to end the shortages of food and consumer goods. To make matters worse, prices of many scarce goods have increased as government price controls have ended.

A City Rich in Culture

Warsaw, Poland's capital and largest city, has more than 1,600,000 people. As the capital, Warsaw is home to many government employees. Their offices are in graceful eighteenth-century buildings. However, the Sejm, Poland's parliament, meets in a modern building.

In Warsaw, the contrast between old and new is dramatic. Nearly all of the city was destroyed during World War II. When the war ended, Warsaw's people faced a huge pile of rubble. Many lived in hastily-built wooden shacks while they began the long process of rebuilding. The beautiful *Stare Miasto*, or "Old Town," which had been perfectly preserved since the thirteenth century, was no more.

The Poles, who loved their Old Town and the traditions it represented, very carefully rebuilt it. They used old photographs and drawings to recreate the Stare Miasto. Today it looks very much as it did hundreds of years ago. Artists display their work in the town square, and some of them live in the beautiful old houses. There are many small restaurants, bars, and *kawiarnie*—cafes where coffee, cake, and snacks are served. Horse-drawn carriages take people on leisurely, romantic rides through the narrow streets.

Warsaw is also a very modern city. Most of its people live in concrete skyscrapers surrounded by lawns and gardens. Downtown, the Centrum Complex of stores, offices, and high-rise apartments is crowded with people hurrying from place to place. Much of Warsaw looks as though it sprang up suddenly in the late 1950s and early 1960s—as indeed it did. Construction has continued since the first burst of rebuilding, though not fast enough to meet all of the city's housing needs. But even in

Zanmek, or the Royal Castle, lies to the right in Warsaw's Stare Miasto. Destroyed in 1944, it was rebuilt with contributions from Poles around the world.

Warsaw's modern sections, there are sad reminders of the past. Plaques, many decorated with fresh flowers, mark where Poles were killed during World War II.

Other Great Cities

On the Baltic coast is Gdansk, another city almost completely destroyed during World War II. Today the city's tall church towers and decorative housetops have been restored. For centuries Gdansk has been a major European port and shipbuilding city. On any day in the harbor, dozens of giant ships fly the flags of many nations. Others are up in dry dock, where workers scrape off barnacles or apply a new coat of paint.

Gdansk is important to Polish history—in 1980, Solidarity, Eastern Europe's first trade union, was founded there. But many of the signs carved into the stone walls of its old buildings are not in Polish, but in German. The city, called Danzig by Germans, was part of Germany throughout much of its past. Gdansk has been the subject of many arguments, and even war, between countries. However, in 1990, Germany officially recognized the borders formed by World War II, and gave up any historical claim to Gdansk and other contested areas.

Every year, thousands of Catholic Poles travel to Czestochowa, many on foot, for a special festival in honor of a famous painting, *Our Lady of Czestochowa.*

The Black Madonna *on display at the Church of the Holy Cross.*
The heart of Chopin, a Polish-born composer, is buried here.

This picture of Mary holding baby Jesus is called *The Black Madonna* because age has darkened the faces of mother and child. It is more than five hundred years old. In 1655, Swedish armies threatened to take over Poland. According to legend, the painting caused them to retreat the day after Christmas.

Poland's oldest city is Krakow. For more than five hundred years, this southern city was the capital of Poland. Wawel Castle, built in the 1360s, was the home of many Polish kings and queens. The Jagiellonian University was founded by King Kazimierz the Great in 1364.

Unlike most other Polish cities devastated by World War II, Krakow's historic buildings are original, not rebuilt. The wartime German military commanders loved Krakow so much that they made it their headquarters. As a result, the city suffered very little damage during World War II.

Near Krakow, in Wieliczka, is a gigantic salt mine. Miners take elevators which plunge hundreds of feet down into the ground. Visitors to the salt mines can see underground rooms covered with salt crystals, statues carved from salt, and a huge ballroom with sparkling salt chandeliers, salt furniture, and shiny polished salt walls. The salt mine also contains a special hospital room for patients with asthma. They can breathe more easily in the salty underground air.

The Tatrys

Krakow is near some of Poland's most beautiful countryside. Although most of Poland is flat, in the south the Carpathian Mountains rise along the Polish-Czechoslovakian border. A popular resort area within the Carpathians is the Tatry Mountains, the highest peaks of which are topped with snow year round. Zakopane, a small city in the mountains, is an important tourist center.

In the Tatrys, the native *gorale* (mountaineers) have a culture and history all their own. Many of them live in wooden cabins just as their ancestors did. On holidays, gorale men wear traditional dress—baggy trousers, boots, and wide leather belts—and carry long-stemmed hatchets called *siekierki*.

In the past, these hatchets were used as weapons. Now they are props in lively dances, where the men jump back and forth over their siekierki handles with breathtaking speed, or toss and stamp their hatchets in rhythm. The energetic dances and wild, harsh music of the gorale are popular throughout Poland.

Historic Regions

Poles may sometimes refer to themselves as gorale, Mazurians (Mazuria is a northeastern section of Poland), Silesians (southwestern), Galicians (southeastern), or

Skiers waltz down the slopes overlooking Zakopane. The Tatry Mountains rise in the background.

Kasubians (from a northwestern section near Germany where most people speak both German and Polish). Or they may say they come from *Malopolska* (Little Poland, a part of Galicia) or *Wielkopolska* (Great Poland, a central area which was once independent). Locating all these places can be a bit confusing. Poland's boundaries have changed so often that its regions cannot be clearly defined on a map!

Today, these regions are not used for legal, official purposes the way states in the United States or provinces in Canada are. But the fact that people often think of themselves as natives of these historic regions shows how important tradition can be to the Poles. Their different heritages can also lead to friendly arguments—for example, about which group pronounces words in the "most Polish" way.

The regional rivalries among Poles are very friendly compared with the disagreements between ethnic groups faced by many of Poland's neighbors. Different ethnic groups within Czechoslovakia and Yugoslavia have often been violently opposed to one another, and some would now like to establish independent states. Poland has had an easier time because, since 1945, nearly all of its people have been ethnic Poles who have believed in the unity of Poland.

Whatever their disagreements, Poles agree on one thing—they're proud to be Polish. They have kept their own ways no matter what other nations have officially controlled them, and no matter what difficulties they have faced. Perhaps the fact that being Polish hasn't always been easy is one reason Poles stick together in loving their land!

2. A Romantic, Religious People

What makes Poles Polish? That is a question that probably cannot be answered completely. But in a room full of Poles, there would be plenty of opinions!

Poles are known for being individuals who don't like being told what to think or what to do. Poles are proud of this independence. Perhaps it comes from the long struggle to keep Polish ways even when outsiders were trying to prevent them from doing so. Yet when they criticize themselves, they often say that this very independence makes it hard to work together. If people are busy arguing about their different opinions, nothing will get done!

Poles, however, have a reputation for being honest, hard workers. They are also known for loving their homes and lands and for taking good care of them. Many Poles save money for buying property, even if they have to give up other pleasures to do it.

Romanticism

Those are all practical qualities. Yet throughout their history, Poles have also been called "romantic." In times of war, Polish soldiers and civilians were willing to face almost any danger to fight for Poland. Even if there were

Young members of the Polish Underground surround the grave of their leader in 1944.

only a few Poles, they were often willing to fight huge enemy armies to preserve Poland's independence.

The Polish people are sometimes called romantic because of their artistic nature. They have long expressed strong feelings of love, beauty, and patriotism through the fine arts.

In modern Poland, the arts are an important part of people's lives. In the cities, many Poles go to theaters, concerts, and movies. Films by Andrzej Wajda and other Polish directors often win prizes at world film festivals. Poster art is also very popular. Polish poster art is often considered the best in the world. A museum near Warsaw displays some of the finest examples.

In the country, folk artists practice crafts that have been passed down over many generations. They weave rugs and wall hangings, carve wood, sew traditional Polish costumes, and make *wycinanki*—paper cutout designs. Many years ago, people used sheep shears to make these cutouts. Today they usually use smaller scissors. Polish folk artists are often farmers who work on their art in the winter. The government pays them to make their art, and it is sold in folk art stores called *Cepelia*.

Famous Poles

Poland's past is full of talented people in the fine arts. Fryderyk (Frederic) Chopin, one of the most famous

Fryderyk Chopin.

musicians who ever lived, was a Pole. He was a pianist and a composer in the 1800s. Along with Brahms, Liszt, Schubert, and others of his time, Chopin was known as a Romantic composer. His music, almost all of which was written for solo piano, is bittersweet—both happy and sad at the same time. Although he lived most of his life in Paris, Chopin never lost his love for Poland. He often used Polish folk melodies and dances—such as the polonaise—in his music.

Other important Polish musicians of the past include Stanislaw Moniuszko. His opera, *Halka*, tells the sad story of a peasant girl who falls in love with a nobleman. Ignacy Paderewski was a pianist who was well known throughout the world and especially in the United States. Karol Szymanowski was one of the earliest composers of modern classical music. Witold Lutoslawski and Krzystof Penderecki are among the world's best-known living classical composers.

In the theater, Helena Modrzejewska (who used the name Modjeska when she performed) was one of the world's most famous actresses in the 1800s. She often had roles in productions of Shakespeare's plays, and gave many performances in North America. In modern times, the mime theater (mime is acting without words) of Henryk Tomaszewski and the experimental theater of Jerzy Grotowski have become well known.

Poland has had many writers. Some are known only in Poland, but others are well known in many countries. Long ago, in the 1500s, Jan Kochanowski was one of the most well known poets in both Latin and Polish. Some of his best and saddest poems are about the death of his young daughter, Orszula.

Does Joseph Conrad sound like a Polish name? How about Jozef Konrad Korzeniowski? That was the original name of Joseph Conrad, the famous writer of "The Heart of Darkness," *Lord Jim,* and other stories and novels, who lived from 1857 to 1924. Although Polish was his native language, he wrote his novels in English.

Three Polish authors have won the Nobel Prize for literature. Henryk Sienkiewicz won it in 1905 for *Quo Vadis,* a popular novel on life in ancient Rome. In 1924, Wladyslaw Reymont won for his novel, *The Peasants,* a four-part story about the lives of Polish country people throughout the four seasons of the year. And in 1980, the poetry of Czeslaw Milosz won the Nobel Prize and has since become quite well known in the United States.

Polish Discoveries

Polish scientists have made important contributions as well. Poland's two most famous scientists lived at very different times.

In the early 1500s, most people thought the sun traveled around the earth. But Mikolaj Kopernik, *Copernicus* in Latin, studied the stars and planets and decided that the sun must be the center of the Solar System, with the earth traveling around it. He wrote a book about his ideas, but did not publish it until just before he died because it challenged church teachings. Later, other scientists studied his book and proved he was right.

Marja (Marie) Sklodowska Curie lived from 1867 to 1934. She was a chemist and a physicist at a time when it was very difficult for female scientists to find jobs. She and her French husband, Pierre Curie, worked together

Marie Curie in her laboratory.

and discovered two new radioactive elements, radium and polonium. Polonium is named after Poland. The Curies won a Nobel Prize for their discoveries in 1903. After Pierre died a few years later, Marja continued to teach and do research in Paris. She won a second Nobel Prize in 1911 for discovering a way to make pure radium.

Poland has had other important scientists. Ignacy Lukasziewicz, the first scientist to drill an oil well, lived in the mid-1800s. He also invented the kerosene lamp. These lamps were an important form of lighting before the electric light bulb, and are still used by campers and travelers. Kazimierz Funk, who lived from 1884 to 1967, discovered and named the first vitamins.

A Polish Pope

The most famous Pole alive today is Karol Wojtyla— Pope John Paul II. He was born in 1920 in Wadowice, a small town not far from Krakow. Young Karol was an athletic boy who liked to dance and play soccer. As a young man, he studied Polish literature and acted in plays at the Jagiellonian University in Krakow. During World War II, when the Nazis occupied Poland and killed many of its people, Karol studied secretly to become a priest.

Wojtyla served the churches of Krakow for more than thirty years—first as a priest, later as the bishop and archbishop of Krakow, and finally as a cardinal. He was known for being warm and friendly, and also for speaking out firmly and clearly about church policies.

In October 1978, Karol Wojtyla was elected pope by all the cardinals of the Roman Catholic church. People everywhere were surprised because, since 1523, only Italians had been chosen as the pope. Karol Wojtyla was the first Polish Pope ever. The Polish people were overjoyed. Pope John Paul II, as he was now called,

Pope John Paul II makes a new friend during his travels.

visited Poland several times—including trips in 1979, 1983, and again in 1987. Each time millions of Poles have turned out to see him.

Poles are very happy and proud to have a Polish pope, because the Roman Catholic church has been very important in their history. At times when other countries controlled Poland, Catholic churches helped Poles keep their language, culture, and religion alive. Today, nearly 90 percent of Poles are Catholics.

People of other religions have been important to Poland, too. Before the Nazi concentration camps of World War II, nearly 10 percent of Poland's citizens were Jews. Some Poles are Protestants, and others are members of the Polish National Catholic church. This religious group broke away from the Roman Catholic church in the United States and was brought to Poland by Polish Americans. A small number of Poles do not belong to a religious group.

The Catholic church is so much a part of Polish traditions that it remained strong even under the Communist government. Many Communist governments banned or put restrictions on the practice of religion. In Poland, Catholicism and communism coexisted. Church and government leaders usually met to discuss problems, even when they strongly disagreed. Many Polish Communists are also Catholics. Catholic magazines have been published in Poland for many years. In addition,

Poland has the only university in Eastern Europe that is run by a religious group—the Catholic University of Lublin.

Speaking *Po Polsku*

No one could describe what makes Poles Polish without mentioning their language. When people who do not speak Polish see a word like *przepraszam* (excuse me) or *szczesliwy* (happy), they sometimes wonder how anyone manages to learn Polish at all! But the language is not nearly as hard to pronounce as it looks. It's not like English, where *through, though,* and *tough* look a lot alike but sound very different! In Polish, *mie,* or *na,* or even *szcz* will always have the same sound.

The love and pride Poles feel for their language shows how they feel about their country. Poles can have different political opinions, different religious beliefs, and different ideas about many other things. But whether they are Communist or anti-Communist, religious Catholics or not, old or young, all Poles have a common bond—a love for their country. There are dozens of songs about how much Poles love Poland. They are often sung whenever people with *polskie sercy* (Polish hearts) get together.

3. Preserving Poland

Legend says that Poland began when a tribe led by three brothers, Lech, Czech, and Rus, wandered into a beautiful land. Lech (whose name is an ancient word for Poland) looked up and saw an eagle in its nest. He came to a decision, saying "This is where we should stay." His brothers argued with him. Finally, the tribe split into three groups: Czech's group went west to Czechoslovakia; Rus's went east to Russia; and Lech's stayed. Lech's people started a city named Gniezno (Nest), and made the white eagle their symbol. Poland was born.

No one knows exactly how Poland really began, but scientists do know that people lived in a cave near Krakow about 18,000 years ago. Remains of a more "modern" village, Biskupin (about 2,700 years old), were discovered and rebuilt near Poznan. About one thousand people lived there in wooden houses and raised grain and animals. The earliest known Polish settlers were Slavic tribes whose language later developed into Polish.

The Piast Kings

Poland's written history began in 966, when Mieszko, a prince of the ruling Piast family, married a Czech princess,

Dubrawa. Dubrawa's home, Bohemia, had already become a Roman Catholic country. Mieszko became a Christian and made all of Poland Christian as well. Until that time, the Poles had believed in spirits of the household and nature.

Mieszko's decision was important to Poland's development for several reasons. By joining the Roman Catholic Church of the West instead of the Eastern Orthodox Christian Church adopted by Russia, Poland had more in common with Western Europe than with lands to the east. Mieszko also avoided an attack from Germany, a Christian land. The Germans would have liked to make Poland a Christian country by force so that they could control it.

The Piast family ruled Poland until 1370. During the 1100s and 1200s, Poland was divided into four kingdoms, each ruled by a different member of the Piast family. These kingdoms frequently squabbled and were often invaded by outsiders, including the Tartars from Asia, the Lithuanians from the northeast, and the Teutonic Knights (a German group) from the west.

Finally, King Wladyslaw the Short brought many parts of Poland back together again in 1320. His son, Kazimierz, became one of Poland's greatest kings. During his reign, from 1333 to 1370, Kazimierz the Great made Poland larger and stronger. But he was much more than a military leader. He also reformed the laws, started a

A Polish eagle crafted in gold in 1595. An eagle used to be on Poland's flag. However, now it is often seen as a symbol of imperialism or communism.

In Krakow and surrounding villages, festivals feature people dressed as the Tartars did during the 1200's.

single system of money, and built so many buildings that it was said of him, "He found a Poland made of wood and left behind one made of stone."

Kazimierz passed laws that protected the common people and provided food during hard times. Some of his new laws protected Jews, who were often cruelly treated in other parts of Europe. In addition, he gave more rights to the nobles and to the towns than most other kings. And, in 1364, he founded the University of Krakow, which still exists today as the Jagiellonian University.

Kazimierz was the last Piast king. Although he was married three times, he did not have any children. However, his sister and her husband, the king of Hungary, had three daughters. Finally it was decided that the youngest daughter, Jadwiga, would become queen of Poland.

Jagiellonian Dynasty

Jadwiga was only ten years old when she was sent away from her family to become queen in far-off Poland. When Jadwiga was twelve, her relatives and the Polish nobles argued about whom she should marry. Jadwiga wanted to marry an Austrian prince. But the Polish nobles did not want the Austrians to gain power in Poland. They wanted her to marry Jagiello, a Lithuanian prince more than twenty years older than she. If Poland and Lithuania united, they would be a very strong kingdom. Finally, to help Poland's future, she agreed.

Queen Jadwiga was admired by her husband and the Polish people. Even Poland's enemies liked her! Much to her people's sorrow, Jadwiga died in childbirth in 1399, when she was only twenty-five.

Jagiello's family continued to rule Poland for almost two hundred years. Not long after the death of Jadwiga,

After the Battle of Grunwald in 1410, the Polish-Lithuanian Kingdom began its Golden Age. At the time of Columbus's first voyage to America, it was one of the largest and most powerful kingdoms in Europe.

a terrible war was fought between the Polish-Lithuanian kingdom and the Teutonic Knights. The Polish side won the war at the Battle of Grunwald in 1410. This victory helped Poland become one of the strongest and largest kingdoms in Europe for several centuries.

The Golden Age

The period from the late 1400s to the early 1600s is known as Poland's Golden Age. Throughout Europe interest in the fine arts, education, and human rights was growing. This time was called the Renaissance, or "rebirth," and Poland played an important role in it.

Poland was known as a country where freedom of thought was protected. Artists were encouraged, and poetry, painting, architecture, and music were popular with the nobles and the middle class. Science became more important, too. This was the time that Mikolaj Kopernik—Copernicus—was studying astronomy.

Freedom of religion was also protected in Poland. During the 1200s, the leaders of the Catholic church in Spain and other countries had a group of investigators known as the Inquisition. For several centuries, it was very dangerous to disagree with the leaders of the Roman Catholic church. Jews and other non-Christians were forced to convert to Christianity, or lose their lives. Protestants and Catholics who opposed official church policies were arrested, tortured, and often killed. Poland's rulers and church leaders, however, refused to allow the Inquisition. People came from all over Europe to seek protection in Poland.

Nobles and Neighbors

During the centuries of Jagiellonian rule, the Polish nobles had gained more and more power. They had formed a parliament, the Sejm. Even though the Jagiello family had passed the crown from father to son, the nobles had the right to vote to approve each king.

Zygmunt August died childless in 1572—ending the Jagiellonian dynasty. This power void allowed the nobles to use their power even more than before. For the next 222 years, they elected Poland's kings.

Poland grew larger. In the early 1600s, the nation stretched from the Baltic Sea to the Black Sea—three times as much land as it has today. But long wars with Sweden, Turkey, and Russia were very hard on Poland.

At the end of the 1600s, the Polish king, Jan Sobieski, was a hero in Western Europe because he kept the Turks from winning European lands. Yet the wars had killed thousands of people, destroyed towns, and made the country weaker. The next two kings elected after Jan Sobieski's death did little to help the Polish people. In fact, they spent more time in their original home, Saxony, than in Poland.

In 1764, Stanislaw Poniatowski, a Polish noble, was elected king. A great friend of the arts, Poniatowski held famous "Thursday dinners" at his palace, where people talked about art, books, and ideas. He also built many beautiful buildings in Warsaw, Poland's capital.

The Polish Constitution

Stanislaw Poniatowski was king at the same time that the American colonies were fighting for independence from

England. Some of the same ideas about freedom and human rights that excited the colonies were also popular in Poland. The Poles created a new constitution that gave more people the right to vote, guaranteed freedoms, and changed some of the rules of government.

One important change was the end of the "liberum veto." This rule had allowed any noble in the Sejm to keep any law from being passed just by standing up and saying "*nie pozwalam*" ("I disapprove"). It was very hard to pass any laws at all when even one liberum veto could stop everything.

Poland's neighbors—Russia, Prussia, and Austria —knew that the old system made the Polish government weak. They wanted the government to stay that way so they could take over Polish land. In fact, the three neighbors had agreed on a treaty four years earlier that gave themselves pieces of Poland! This takeover of land is known as the First Partition of Poland.

When the new constitution was announced, the Russian czar, or ruler, ordered the Poles to give it up. When Poland refused, Russia invaded. Poland lost the fight, and the Russians took most parts of the eastern section of the Polish-Lithuanian kingdom. The Prussians (Germans) took some western land, including the city of Gdansk (Danzig). This was the Second Partition of Poland.

Finally, Tadeusz Kosciuszko —who had helped the Americans during the revolution—led a revolution against

The First Partition, 1772. Poland lost about a third of its land to the neighboring countries of Austria, Russia, and Prussia (Germany).

The Second Partition, 1793. Prussia took most of western Poland while Russia took much of what is now the Ukraine and Lithuania.

the new Russian rule. The Poles fought bravely, but eventually they lost. In 1795, Russia, Prussia, and Austria forced King Stanislaw Poniatowski to resign and divided the rest of Poland among themselves. Suddenly, with the Third Partition, Poland had disappeared from the map.

Poland Disappears— and Returns

Although legally there was no country named Poland for 123 years, Poland did not vanish from the hearts and minds of the Poles. Even with their nation divided into three pieces, Poles continued to keep Polish ways, use the Polish language, express their heritage through the arts, and hope for the rebirth of their land. They did so even though there were laws against speaking Polish and keeping Polish ways in the Russian and Prussian sections of their country.

The Third Partition, 1795. Russia, Prussia, and Austria divide up Poland. Poland ceases to be an independent country.

In 1914, World War I began. The Austrians and Prussians fought on one side, and the Russians fought on the opposite side (with France, England, and eventually the United States). As a result, Poles drafted into one country's army had to fight Poles in the opposing army. Poles all hoped that the end of the war would bring about an independent Poland. However, they disagreed about which side was likely to win, and about how to get support for the reunification of Poland.

When the long, costly war finally ended, Poles found that setting up a new Poland was not easy. Every country had its own ideas about how to redraw the map of Europe, and Poland did not get all the land it wanted. Also, the Russian czar had just been overthrown by a new Communist government, which did not send anyone to the peace treaty meetings. That meant Poland's eastern boundary was unclear.

In the new Poland's first eight years, it had thirteen different governments. Finally, Jozef Pilsudski, a Polish general, took over the government and stayed in charge until he died in 1935. To some Poles, Pilsudski was a selfish man who wanted too much power. To others, he was the strong leader they felt Poland needed, and a hero.

Life in the new Poland was hard for most Poles. There were fights with neighbors over boundary lines, including a war with Russia in 1920. Many people were poor, and prices for everyday items skyrocketed. In 1919, it took twelve Polish marks to equal one American dollar. But seven years later, one dollar was worth six million marks!

Still, the Poles worked hard to rebuild the cities and factories the war had destroyed. They passed new laws so that farmers would have enough land. They started a new, stronger bank with a new kind of money, the *zloty*, to try to reduce inflation. And they greatly improved their system of education. By 1920, 95 percent of Polish children were in school, more than in many other nations.

A Painful War

The Polish people wanted peace and time to build their new nation. But by the 1930s, the whole world was going through a difficult period. The Great Depression made life hard for millions of people who were out of work. In many European countries, dictators took power away from elected governments. Dictators are rulers who hold complete control over their people.

In the Soviet Union, Josef Stalin was the dictator. During his reign (1929-1953), he arrested millions of people whom he considered enemies. Many were killed, and many more were sent to labor prison camps in Siberia. Even some Polish Communists, who had thought the Soviets would be their friends, were arrested.

In Germany, Adolf Hitler was dictator from 1933 to

*Wartime Polish refugees prepare to leave Warsaw. The Nazis
"resettled" many Poles so Germans could move in.*

1945. Like Stalin, he was an extremely cruel ruler. Since
both dictators wanted to make their countries larger, they
made secret plans to invade Poland and take Polish land.
Britain and France had pledged to defend Poland, but
Hitler didn't think that they would stand up to him. On
September 1, 1939, Hitler's armies invaded Poland from
the west. It was a terrible surprise for Poland, and caused
the beginning of World War II. Only two weeks later,

Jews being deported from Lodz to a concentration camp in 1943. Three million Polish Jews died in these camps.

Stalin's armies invaded Poland from the east. Once again, Poland's neighbors had divided the country.

World War II was one of the worst times in Polish history. Poland was controlled by the Nazis, Hitler's forces, for six long years. Much of the country was destroyed. One-fifth of Poland's population, more than six million people—including three million Jews—were killed. Many died in battles and bombings.

However, millions of people from Poland and other parts of Europe also died in Nazi concentration camps. Since Hitler wanted to destroy the Jewish people, millions of these prisoners were Jews. Many non-Jewish Poles, especially well-educated ones who opposed Hitler, were also arrested. One of the worst Nazi concentration camps was Auschwitz in southern Poland. Today it is a memorial to the 4 million people from seventeen nations who were killed there.

Although it was very dangerous, secret groups met in Poland during the war to resist the Nazis and support the Allies. The allied nations included France, England, and the United States. In 1941, the Soviet Union also joined the Allies, because Germany broke its agreement and invaded it.

Finally, in 1945, the Allies won the war. Once again, countries met to draw a new map of Europe, and once more, Poland's boundaries caused arguments.

4. Fighting to be Free

Today's Poland does not include exactly the same land as the Poland of 1918 to 1939. Some eastern land was made part of the Soviet Union after World War II, and some western land that had been part of Germany was made part of Poland. Many people, both German and Polish, had to move after the war. To keep living in their homelands, they had to leave their homes.

The Poles had a huge rebuilding project. The country had very little money, and many were homeless and hungry. They rebuilt their cities, but the Poles also had to rebuild their government. The late 1940s were a confusing time, especially since several different groups claimed to be the "true" Polish government.

Communist Domination

After World War II, the Soviet Union developed a sphere of influence—an area that it controlled—throughout what we now call Eastern Europe. East Germany, Romania, Czechoslovakia, Hungary, Bulgaria, and Poland, as well as Yugoslavia for awhile, all became Soviet *satellites*. These countries were politically and economically controlled by the U.S.S.R.

After World War II, Russia, combined with the republics it controlled (in red), was known as the U.S.S.R. It gradually gained control of the governments of Eastern Europe, (in yellow).

The Soviet Union wanted to make sure the new Poland would be its ally—and under its control. Stalin's supporters were active in Poland. Poles who were against Soviet control asked for help from England, France, and the United States—but they did not get very much. Eventually, the U.S.S.R. stopped nearly all contact between the East and the West. Distrust grew. The Cold War, as this period of history is known, had begun. It would last for several decades.

Most Poles were not Communists and did not want a Communist government, especially one controlled by the Soviets. Interference from Russians is especially unwelcome to Poles because the two peoples have a long history of problems.

For the first few years, there was a coalition government which included non-Communists and others that disagreed with Stalin. But by 1948, Stalin's supporters had complete control.

The period from 1948 to 1954 was a difficult one. Stalin was a harsh dictator, and tightly controlled the arts, the press, speech, and religion. Catholic bishops and even Poland's Cardinal Wyszynski were arrested. Soviet troops and military police stayed in Poland to keep control. Soviets were given important government jobs. Poland was also forced to sell farm and industrial products to the Soviet Union for very low prices. As a result, Poland did not make enough money for its own needs.

After Stalin died in 1953, changes slowly began. In 1956, the new Soviet leader, Nikita Khrushchev, made a speech that criticized Stalin's cruelty. The same year, in Poznan, Poland, workers rioted to protest the lack of freedom and lack of consumer goods.

The Polish Road

Wladyslaw Gomulka, a Polish Communist who had been arrested by Stalin's government for his belief that Poland should have more independence, became the new head of

The Palace of Culture—built in the Stalinist style—is a symbol of the Communist era to many in Poland.

the government. When Gomulka took over, Soviet troops started moving toward Poland. Since the Soviet troops had just fought Hungarians who had tried to change their government, many people feared that the same thing would happen in Poland.

Instead, Gomulka and Khrushchev reached an agreement. Poland promised to support the Soviet Union in all foreign policy and make sure the Communist party stayed in charge of Poland. But, Poland could take the "Polish road to socialism" instead of copying the Soviet plan exactly. Farmers were allowed to keep their private land instead of losing it to collective farms. There was more freedom of speech and freedom to travel. Also, the Catholic church could carry on its work.

The Balancing Act

After the "Polish October," as this agreement was called, in 1956, Poland had to balance several needs at once. During the decades when Soviet Communists dominated Eastern Europe, Poland was in an especially delicate position. As a military and trade ally of the U.S.S.R., Poland had to support Soviet foreign policies even when the Poles disagreed with them. The Polish Communist government did allow more liberties to its own people than the Soviet government did in the U.S.S.R. Still, it was always important to avoid going "too far." The Poles feared that if they passed too many reforms, the Soviet Union might invade Poland or interfere in other ways.

Protests and Improvements

In 1970, an increase in food prices was announced at a time when the economy was already bad. There were many protests. Some were peaceful, but in the northern coast cities of Gdansk, Gdynia, Sopot, and Szczecin, people fought in the streets with soldiers. Some of the protesters were killed, and Gomulka had to leave office.

The new Polish leader was Edward Gierek, a former miner. He met with workers, raised wages, allowed more consumer goods to be produced, and gave more government money for travel and study in other countries. In many ways, life was good during the 1970s. The economy grew, travel was easier, and the arts were encouraged.

Unfortunately, Poland also borrowed a great deal of foreign money. When the world economy grew worse in the early 1980s, Poland's debts were so large that they could not be paid. People had to wait in line again, even to buy basic foods. Once again, the Poles were angry.

These problems led to the formation of *Solidarnosc* (Solidarity trade union) in 1980 and 1981. This was the first time a Communist country in Eastern Europe had a trade union that was not controlled by the government. Soon Solidarnosc members went on strike to protest the things they wanted changed.

The new union's leader, Lech Walesa, was a shipyard worker in Gdansk. Some people in the government and the union tried to turn peaceful Solidarity demonstrations into violent ones. But Walesa believed that peace was the only good way to make changes. "Peaceful change takes longer, but it is more successful," he said. Soon he was a

Outlawed Solidarity members demand international attention as they greet the Pope in 1987. Their signs call for elections and peace.

popular man not only in Poland, but throughout the world. In 1983, he won a Nobel Peace Prize.

Many Poles agreed with Walesa, but there were some who did not. Some members of Solidarnosc thought changes should be made quickly. They wanted to force the government to meet their demands. Some government members thought change was happening too fast and wanted to outlaw Solidarity. There was always the fear that the Soviet Union would invade Poland if the strikes continued, or if the Polish Communist party seemed to be losing power.

Martial Law

During this troubled time, there were several changes of leadership. General Wojciech Jaruzelski finally took control, and on December 13, 1981, he declared martial law—a state of emergency where the army has complete control of the country.

Poles disagree about why Jaruzelski declared martial law. Some believe he was acting under orders from the Soviet Union. Others believe he decided that martial law run by Poles was the only way to keep the Soviet Union from invading Poland.

Under martial law, the armed forces were in control, and freedoms were limited. Some people were arrested, and others, such as Lech Walesa, were put under house arrest. Under house arrest, a person is not kept in jail, but he or she cannot come and go without permission.

The Polish government announced that it would end martial law on National Day, July 22, 1983. The leaders had already asked the Sejm to pass new laws that would give the government more control over political and work activities. The Sejm passed some, but not all, of these laws. Solidarity, however, was declared illegal and new unions were set up that were under government control.

Throughout the 1980s, the Polish economy remained slow. Although Solidarity was illegal, union members continued to meet, publish materials, and even carry Solidarnosc signs at times.

A Time of Rapid Change

In the mid-1980s, a change in leadership in the Soviet Union began to affect all of Eastern Europe. Mikhail Gorbachev became general secretary of the Soviet Communist party in 1985. Three years later, he was named president of the U.S.S.R. As he gained power, Gorbachev stressed new ideas of openness and international cooperation. Freedom of speech and of the press improved in many Eastern nations. The Berlin Wall that separated East and West Germany came down, and the two parts of Germany reunited in 1990. Relations between the East and West improved. After forty years of tensions and threats, the Cold War came to an end.

These new Soviet policies were welcomed by Poles. In fact, Poland became a leader in making many changes that soon swept through Eastern Europe. In January 1989, the Polish Communist party leaders finally agreed to hold talks with Solidarity. On April 5, Solidarity was declared legal again. General elections were held on June 4. These were the freest elections held in Poland in fifty years. Candidates supported by Solidarity won many seats in the lower house of the Sejm, and ninety-nine of the one hundred seats in the newly formed upper house.

In July, Jaruzelski was elected president of Poland. In August, Tadeusz Mazowiecki, an important Solidarity leader, became prime minister. A coalition government that included both Communist and non-Communist members was formed.

However, by September, Lech Walesa announced that he planed to run for president. Jaruzelski agreed to step down in favor of the winner of these elections. Six candidates, including both Lech Walesa and Tadeusz Mazowiecki, ran for president on November 25. Since no candidate won a majority, the top two candidates ran in a second election December 9. Many people were surprised that Walesa's opponent in the December election was not Mazowiecki, but a Polish-born Canadian businessman, Stanislaw Tyminski. However, Walesa

Walesa is pleased by the round table talks in May 1989, because the government agreed to many of Solidarity's demands.

won easily, capturing 77 percent of the vote. He became President of the Republic of Poland in December, 1990.

Poland's new government faces many old challenges, especially the need to improve and strengthen the economy. Poland's dramatic shift to a market economy, known as the "Big Bang," has pioneered the way for Eastern European countries to join Western markets. Even the Soviet Union has followed the Polish example.

The majority of Poles favor the shift to a market economy. But the changes so far have raised prices, increased housing costs by an average of 75 percent, and created previously unknown unemployment. These developments have not been welcomed by a people already tired of shortages and debts.

Political Questions

The continuing economic difficulties, and the increased competition among political groups, have led to many political disagreements in 1990. Many people believe that communism has become so unpopular in Poland that it will lose all of its influence in a few years. Political and economic changes have also increased the conflicts within Solidarity. For example, Lech Walesa and Tadeusz Mazowiecki, once close allies, publicly disagreed about a number of government decisions in 1990.

Some Poles say they are tired of both communism and Solidarity, and are looking for new parties and new ideas. Some predict that Solidarity will split into several parties. Others believe that the movement will become stronger once genuine economic growth begins.

Improving the economy will not be easy, but many Poles hope that their newly formed democratic society will make it less difficult. Western Europe, the United States, and international organizations such as the World

Bank have been more interested in giving Poland loans and financial aid—but so far they have done little. Poles hope that increased trade and new private businesses will help the country grow. Once the economy is strengthened by close ties to Western Europe, Poland may eventually join the European Community.

The 1990s are full of challenges for Poles as they struggle to cope with great political and economic changes. No one thinks these changes will be achieved without going through hard times. But Poles are excited by their increased independence, and difficulties have not stopped this determined people in the past.

5. Kings and Queens, Knights and Dragons

Poland has many legends and stories about the past. No one knows how old these legends are, because Poles have been telling them for hundreds of years—maybe even thousands of years!

Some stories explain natural features of Poland. For example, Poland is well known for its amber, a clear golden "stone" that is actually the hardened sap of prehistoric trees. It is used to make necklaces and other jewelry. The scientific explanation of amber isn't the only one. There is also the story of the Queen of the Baltic.

Queen of the Baltic

The Queen of the Baltic was a very beautiful woman who lived in a huge, amber castle at the bottom of the sea. She took care of all the fish and other creatures who lived in the sea. When she ate fish for dinner, she would eat only half of each one and use her magic to allow the other half to swim away unharmed. These funny-looking half-fish are today's flounder.

The queen was loved by the god of thunder and lightning, who protected her castle from storms. One day,

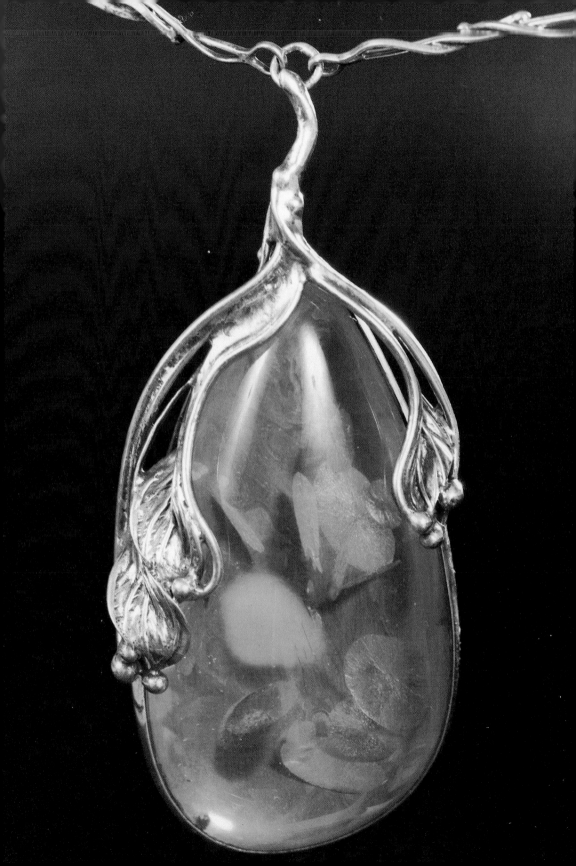

the Queen of the Baltic heard of a handsome young fisherman who was setting traps. The queen swam to shore meaning to scold the fisherman, but instead fell in love with him. The fisherman returned her love, and every day they would meet on the shore of the Baltic.

The thunder god grew jealous. One night when the queen returned from her visit to the fisherman, the thunder god started a terrible storm. He struck her amber castle with a huge bolt of lightning, killed the queen, and broke the castle into millions of pieces. Pieces of amber still wash up on shore from time to time. As for the fisherman, the angry god chained him to the bottom of the ocean. During storms, his moans can still be heard in the wind.

Queen Kinga's Dowry

Another legend, about Queen Kinga's Dowry, explains how the giant salt mine in Wieliczka was made. A Hungarian princess, Kinga, was getting ready for her wedding to the prince of Poland. Her father asked her, "What do you want for your dowry?" A dowry is an expensive present the bride's family gives to the groom. Kinga answered, "I want a salt mine."

Now, to modern people, that sounds like a funny present. But long ago, salt was very valuable because it was the only way people could keep their food fresh. Unfortunately, the king did not have a salt mine. So when

An amber pendant. The objects in the amber were floating in the tree sap before it was petrified.

A salt sculpture on the interior wall of the mine at Wieliczka.

Kinga arrived in Poland, she asked the Polish people if they had ever had one. "Once we had a very small one at Wieliczka, but there is no more salt in it now," they said.

Kinga was determined to see it anyway. As she visited it, she dropped her engagement ring down a mine shaft. She told the people to dig, promising a reward for the person who found her ring. As they started digging, they discovered more salt than they knew what to do with! They brought Kinga a huge salt crystal containing her ring. Queen Kinga was very happy to have her dowry at last.

The Dragon of Krakow

The legend of the Wawel Dragon is one of the most famous myths that tell about Polish history. It is a story that not only tells about the founding of Krakow, but shows that cleverness is more important than power and riches.

Long ago, a huge, mean, horrible dragon lived in southern Poland. When the dragon was hungry, it came down off its hill, burned down barns and houses, and gobbled up the sheep, cattle, or people inside.

The king was so worried about the dragon that he offered a reward to anyone who could kill it: the hand of his daughter in marriage, and the right to be the next king of Poland. Many brave, strong knights tried to fight the dragon. But every time the dragon burned them up before they could get close enough to stab it with their swords.

One day a young shoemaker's son, Krak, came to see the king. "I think I can kill the dragon," said Krak. The king looked doubtful. "But you don't have a sword, or any armor," said the king. He did not know that Krak's plan was to outwit the dragon, not overpower it.

Krak bought a dead ram from a butcher shop. He cut the ram open with his sharp shoemaker's knife and then stuffed it with sulfur, which is used to make matches. Then he sewed the ram up again and stood it outside the dragon's cave.

The dragon couldn't resist a tasty ram. Soon he came out of his lair and swallowed the ram in one gulp. The sulfur mixed with the flames in the dragon's stomach and made a fire so big and hot that the dragon became terribly thirsty. He ran to the river and drank until he could hold no more.

Krak jumped out from his hiding place and teased the dragon. The dragon tried to blow fire at him, but all that came out was steam. As he tried to blow and blow, the dragon filled up with steam until he exploded! At last the people were free.

Krak married the princess, and they built a big castle on the top of the dragon's hill—Wawel Castle. The "dragon's den" can still be seen there today. Krak was a wise, good ruler, and a great city grew around Wawel Castle—the city of Krakow.

The Mouse Tower

The story of Popiel and the Mouse Tower tells about a different kind of legendary rulers, and shows that greed and cruelty are punished. Popiel and his wife, Hilderica, were selfish, mean rulers. They took the people's grain as taxes and stored it in a tower on an island in Lake Goplo. When hard times came the people did not have enough to eat. Yet the evil king and queen refused to give the people any of their food.

Wawel Castle.

Angered by their selfish rulers, the people started scheming to make one of Popiel's brothers king. When Popiel and Hilderica heard of those plans, they invited all the king's brothers to dinner and served them poisoned wine. The brothers died, and the evil king and queen threw their bodies into the lake.

But Popiel and Hilderica did not get away with their crime so easily. All the mice and rats in the city were just as hungry as the people were. They smelled the food at the castle and swarmed towards it. When Popiel and Hilderica saw the rodents coming, they rowed in a little boat to the grain tower on the island, thinking that they would be safe there. But the mice and rats swam onto the island, chewed their way into the tower, and gobbled up all the grain and the evil queen and king with it!

After that, Piast, an honest wheelwright (someone who makes wheels and wagons), was chosen king. He is the legendary ancestor of the Piast kings. Legend also says that the angels came down to visit the early Piasts as a sign that they would found a great nation. Once again, as in the story of Krak, a tradesman of good character defeated the noble-born.

Sleeping Knights

Not all Polish legends are about kings and queens. Some are about other kinds of heroes such as the Sleeping

Knights. These legendary heroes represent Poland's search for freedom.

There are many stories about a group of brave knights who sleep with their chief and their horses in a cave in the Tatry Mountains. Legend says that someday they will wake up and fight for a free Poland. Sometimes ordinary people, or brave Polish knights, wander into a cave and wake them from their long slumber. Then their chief tells them to go back to sleep because it is not yet time to fight for freedom.

One story about the knights tells of a stranger who came into a nearby town and asked a blacksmith to make a golden horseshoe. He took the blacksmith to a cave where the sleeping knights and their horses lay. One of the horses was missing a golden shoe, and the blacksmith replaced it. The stranger gave the blacksmith a big bag of gold but made him promise not to tell anyone about the cave. When the blacksmith returned to the village, he could not keep the secret to himself. He ran to tell his wife and friends, but when he did, the bag of gold turned into a bag of sand. The blacksmith searched and searched for the cave, but he never found it again.

Janosik

Unlike the Sleeping Knights, Janosik was a real person. He was the leader of a band of twelve outlaws in the Tatry

These modern gorale's traditional costumes resemble the clothes of Janosik—especially the belts and hatchets.

Mountains in the early 1700s. Since that time, many of the stories about him have become larger than life.

Janosik was no ordinary outlaw. He was a hero who stole from the rich and gave to the poor mountain people— much like England's Robin Hood. In those days, landlords made the mountain people pay high taxes. When the people could not pay, the landlords would take the people's crops and cattle, making them even poorer.

Legend says that Janosik had superhuman powers, because some witches had given him three magic gifts. He had a wool shirt that would stop bullets and arrows and a red belt that helped him run like the wind. He also carried a special mountaineer's axe that helped him climb any mountain, no matter how steep.

The landlords tried to catch him, and offered big rewards for his capture. But Janosik kept helping the poor. Finally, the landlords offered a huge reward to Janosik's girlfriend. The money was too much to resist.

Janosik's girlfriend waited until he was asleep. Then she stole his magic shirt, belt, and axe and burned them. The fire was also a signal to the rich people, who came and caught Janosik. The real Janosik was executed in 1713. Some say his ghost is still in the mountains, stealing from the rich and giving to the poor.

Pan Twardowski

Not everyone wanted to distribute wealth like Janosik. Pan Twardowski was a nobleman who had, so legends say, spent all his money enjoying himself, but wanted to be rich again. In order to have riches again, he signed a contract with the Devil. It said that when Pan Twardowski went to Rome, which he was planning to do in a few months, the Devil could take his soul. Until then, the Devil had to give him whatever he wanted.

"Ha, ha," said Pan Twardowski after the contract was signed. "Now I will never go to Rome, and you will have to serve me forever!"

Pan Twardowski demanded lots of expensive food and wine, fine clothes, magical powers, rooms full of gold, and everything else anyone had ever desired—even a giant rooster for a steed. The Devil grudgingly gave him everything he requested.

One day, the Devil invited Twardowski to a fine hotel for a delicious dinner. Once they had finished eating, the Devil began to laugh. "Now I've fooled you!" he said as he pointed to the hotel sign. The name of the hotel was "Rome." Since Pan Twardowski was "in Rome," the Devil could take his soul.

The Devil grabbed Twardowski and flew up the chimney into outer space on the way to Hell. Pan Twardowski began to think about how selfish and greedy he had been. He sang a hymn and hoped that the Virgin Mary would help him. Suddenly the Devil vanished. The Virgin Mary had taken pity on Pan Twardowski—but she would not let him into Heaven. Instead, he landed on the moon, where he remains, all alone, to this day.

The Krakow Trumpeter

Another legend based on fact is the story of the Krakow Trumpeter. At Mariacki, the church of Saint Mary in the center of Krakow, there is a very high tower. Long ago, a watchman with a trumpet sat in the tower to watch for danger. If he saw a fire, or any other danger, he blew a trumpet to warn the people of Krakow.

One evening about seven hundred years ago, the whole city was celebrating a holiday. The watchman saw an army of Tartars sneaking into the city. He started playing his alarm, a tune called the "Hejnal," and the townspeople heard the trumpet call just in time. The angry Tartars shot arrows at the trumpeter. One arrow hit him in the throat while he played.

From that time on, the "Hejnal" has been played every hour in the Mariacki tower. But instead of playing the whole tune, the trumpeter stops with a sudden, broken-off high note to mark the spot where the watchman was shot. That way, Poles are always reminded of the young man's bravery.

6. Holiday Times

The Polish calendar is full of holidays, each with its own set of customs and traditions. Many customs are from the time before Poland became a Christian nation. They show the Poles' ancient love for their land, animals, and crops, as well as their feelings about the importance of nature. These ancient customs have been mixed into the holidays of the Roman Catholic church for many centuries. As a result, it is sometimes hard to tell the difference between them and the Christian ones.

Christmas and Easter are the two most important holidays in Poland. Actually, they could be called the two most important holiday seasons, because each holiday has several weeks of traditional customs.

Christmas Gaiety

The Christmas season starts on November 12, the first day of Advent, when Catholics traditionally fast and pray. In Poland, it also used to be the time when people got together for winter work parties. People would pluck feathers for bedding, spin or sew, repair farm tools, or do other indoor work while one person read aloud or told stories.

During Advent, Poles celebrate several special saints' days. Saint Catherine's Day, November 25, and Saint Andrew's Day, November 30, are for parties and dancing. Boys and girls who feel romantic break off a twig from a cherry tree (boys on Saint Catherine's, girls on Saint Andrew's) and put it into a glass of water. If it blooms before New Year's Day, that means success in love for the coming year. Sometimes young people wear the cherry blossoms on New Year's Day or give them to the person they hope will "get the hint"!

At midnight on Saint Andrew's Eve, Poles gather for fortune telling. They pour hot wax into a pan of cold water. The wax hardens into odd shapes as it cools. Each person holds his or her lump of wax in front of a light, so it casts shadows on the wall. The shape of the shadows is said to tell the partygoers what to expect in the new year.

On Saint Nicholas Day, December 6, in the Polish tradition, someone posing as Saint Nicholas dresses as a bishop. This Saint Nicholas arrives in a sleigh with his assistant, who helps him give out presents, religious pictures, and honey cakes for all the good children. Naughty children might get coal instead. However, there are very few naughty children around Saint Nicholas Day!

As Christmas gets closer, groups of people start going from house to house singing Polish songs. Often these carolers carry s*zopka*—puppet theaters—and act out the Christmas story. Naturally, the performers expect to be invited into a home for refreshments whenever they stop to sing or put on a show.

Just before Christmas, Poles break the *oplatek* with family and friends. The oplatek is a thin white wafer, like the ones used for Catholic communion. It often has a Christmas scene stamped on it. When people wish each other a merry Christmas, they break off and eat pieces of each other's oplatek. Some even send pieces of it in Christmas cards to friends and relatives who are far away.

The Wigilia

Finally, the big day comes—Christmas Eve. Everyone works hard all day preparing the *wigilia*, or Christmas Eve dinner. No one can sample any of the food, though, for it is traditional not to eat anything until the first star appears in the sky. The children eagerly scan the sky as it gets dark, each child hoping to be the first to see the star.

Once the family sits down to dinner, they will eat many tasty foods. Baked fish, almond soup, beet soup, cabbage, poppyseed cake, and potato dumplings are all popular wigilia fare, but meat is never served. According to tradition, there must be an odd number of foods, and it is bad luck not to taste every one.

After dinner everyone sings Christmas carols. This is

often the time when families open gifts, too. Santa (called the Star Man in some places) may also visit the children and bring them more gifts—even though they already received some on Saint Nicholas Day.

Christmas Day is usually a quiet holiday with the family. In the days when large Polish houses had servants, December 25 and 26 were holidays for them. For, according to tradition, no one is supposed to do any work, including housekeeping and cooking, on this special day. Although there were many good things to eat, all the food had been cooked before Christmas. Today, Poles do not follow this custom closely.

Polish children and adults often make their own Christmas decorations instead of buying them. Egg shells made into pitchers, doves, and roosters are common decorations along with stars, angels, and glass ornaments. Chains made of fruit, grain, straw, or colored paper are popular, too. Polish homes have Christmas trees, but in some areas, the top of a tree is cut off and hung upside-down from the ceiling instead. It is decorated with ornaments and small gifts and looks much like a regular Christmas tree.

Poles still celebrate Christmas after December 25. Saint Stephen's Day, December 26, and the rest of the days until New Year's, are a time to visit friends and have parties. In fact, a traditional Polish Christmas lasts until Twelfth Night, January 6, or even until Candlemas,

These women present traditional holiday food.

February 2. New Year's Eve is called *Sylvester* in Poland. One important Sylvester custom is to have grand balls, with music and dancing. Another custom is more mischievous: to play a few tricks on friends.

Kings and Kuligs

Twelfth Night, or Epiphany, is the day of the Three Kings. Special church services are held to bless water and chalk. People use this chalk to write "K.M.B." over their doors for good luck. These initials stand for the names of the Three Kings—Kaspar, Melchior, and Balthazar. In some parts of Poland, boys dress up as the Three Kings and go from house to house.

Small cakes and rolls are baked especially for New Year's and Twelfth Night. Often they are baked with coins or almonds in some of them. Whoever gets one of the lucky cakes will know the new year will be a happy one.

After the Christmas season ends, it's only a few months until the Easter season begins. In between, there is another Polish custom—the *kulig*—that can be fun for anyone bored by the winter cold.

Polish nobles who lived in the country started this custom that continues today. One family would get into a sleigh covered with jingle bells, and gallop across the fields to the home of a neighbor. Usually the visit was a

Handmade Christmas ornaments.

surprise, but the neighbor was expected to give everyone lots of food and drink. Then the two families would all go on to a third friend's house for another party. Sometimes the kulig lasted for several days, getting larger and larger with each stop!

Today, kuligs are usually not so long. In the country, people do sometimes still travel by sleigh to their friends' houses. In the city, though, they usually go by car, bus, or trolley.

The Easter Season

The Easter season begins with Carnival, a day for parties before Lent begins. Lent, the forty weekdays before Easter, is a serious time when devoted Christians fast and pray.

Like Catholics in other countries, Polish Catholics have ashes put on their foreheads on Ash Wednesday—the first day of Lent—to show their sadness about Jesus's death. On Good Friday, there are special church services. Some Poles cover their mirrors with black veils on Good Friday. When people look into the mirror, they will see their faces veiled in proper mourning for the death of Christ. Another Good Friday custom in some Polish homes is to wake up the children by tapping them with sticks and saying, "Remember the wounds of Christ." The tapping is in memory of the beating Jesus received from his enemies as he was carrying the cross.

The day before Easter, many Poles take baskets of food to church to have them blessed for Easter dinner. The baskets are often decorated with beautiful hand-embroidered napkins and contain bread, sausage, cakes, eggs, and butter shaped into lambs.

Polish Easter eggs, *pisanki*, are very beautiful. Instead of dyeing the eggs just one color, or even two, the pisanki have many colors and designs. Sometimes hot colored wax is used to make the designs. It takes patience and

Pisanki are painstakingly decorated.

artistic talent to make pisanki. A single mistake could ruin the beautiful pattern!

The pisanki and flowers are used to decorate the tables for Easter dinner. Often the Easter food is placed on a special cloth and displayed on a separate table from the table where the family eats. Stuffed pig's head used to be the traditional main dish. The nobles also drank a special brandy which had bits of real gold floating in it.

Today, Easter dinner still includes pork, as well as sausage, veal, vegetables and soups, bread, eggs, lamb-shaped butter, and plenty of cakes and wine.

Easter Monday is also an important holiday. An interesting custom is *smigus dyngus*. In the gentle form of this custom, boys and men spray water or perfume on the girls and women they know. But there's another way to observe this custom: the boys throw whole buckets of water on the girls! The boys try to take the girls by surprise, but the girls know what to expect and sometimes get the boys wet, too.

Happy Holidays

Although the Christmas and Easter seasons are Poland's most important holidays, they certainly are not the only ones. Poles like to celebrate, and there are many "little" holidays during the year as well as big ones.

Saint John's Eve, also called Sobotka or Swietojanki, is celebrated on June 23, when the days are very long. When the sun finally goes down, single girls and women place flower wreaths and lighted candles on tiny rafts. Then they float the rafts down a stream to waiting young men. A young man who fancies a particular young woman will wade into the stream to try to catch her wreath. If he catches the right raft, it is good luck for their love. If he can catch it without putting the candle out, that

Young dancers perform a harvest dance at a folk festival.

is a sign they will be getting married soon!

Later in the year, there are harvest festivals. August 15 is the day of Our Lady of the Harvest, and all through late August and early September there are harvest parties in different parts of Poland. In the country, people often wear the traditional costumes of their region. They might also wear wreaths on their heads made out of wheat or other grains. August 15 is also Assumption Day, a day to celebrate the Virgin Mary, the mother of Jesus Christ.

Most Polish holidays are so old that no one really knows when they started. But there are some newer, government holidays, too. In Europe, Labor Day is celebrated on May 1 instead of in September. It is an important holiday in Europe, and in Poland there are often formal parades with military marches and speeches by government officials. New holidays might be declared as the new government takes shape.

One type of holiday occurs every day on the Polish calendar—a name day. Each day is the special day of a particular saint. At that time, everyone who has the same name celebrates. Poles named Stanislaw celebrate on Saint Stanislaw's Day, those named Barbara celebrate on Saint Barbara's Day, and so on.

In Poland, a person's name day is much more important than his or her birthday. Young children do celebrate their birthdays, often by bringing cakes or candies to school to share with their friends. But older children and adults have big parties on their name days instead of their birthdays. There are presents, cakes, and other good foods. Everyone sings *"Sto lat, sto lat, niech zyje, zyje nam!"* "May you live for a hundred years!"

7. Friends, Families, and Food

"Gosc w domu, Bog w domu." "A guest in the house is God in the house." That old Polish saying shows how strongly Poles feel about making visitors welcome. Anyone who visits Poland learns that from experience.

Poles will help tourists even if it means going far out of their way. Visitors to Poland often come home with stories about meeting Poles who showed them all over the city, and invited them home for dinner. Then the Poles would call up friends and relatives in other towns who happily offered to do the same thing.

Poles are even more generous to their friends and family. They like to have big parties at holidays, name days, weddings, christenings, and even funerals. When there is no special occasion, Poles still enjoy spending time with their friends and families.

Polish Weddings

Polish weddings are probably the most well known of all Polish celebrations. A hundred years ago, these weddings sometimes lasted a week. Today, a large wedding might mean a weekend of celebrating. This is especially true in the country, where people keep more of the old ways.

To be legally married in Poland, all a couple has to do is go through a short ceremony and sign a form. But almost everyone also has a church wedding with a big reception afterwards. Family and friends come from far away for the wedding, and there is plenty of food, drink, music, and dancing.

There are many old wedding customs, though modern brides and grooms do not usually practice all of them. For example, they often wear white gowns and tuxedos instead of traditional clothing, especially if they live in the city. Still, most Poles do travel to and from the church in horse-drawn carriages or cars decorated with flowers.

Newlyweds are greeted at the door of their new home with bread and salt. The bread is supposed to mean that they will always have plenty to eat. The salt means that they will be wise about spending and saving.

In the country, weddings often follow more of the old ways. Before the wedding, the groom sends the bride liquor. The bride sends large, flat cakes to her family and friends to announce the wedding.

On their wedding day, the bride and groom wear the colorful clothing of their region. The bride has a wreath of flowers and ribbons on her head. Both bride and groom are dressed by their friends for the big event. When the groom is ready, his friends and family, plus some musicians, gather into a big parade. They first go to the bride's house, and then to the church. Everyone sings

People at Polish weddings often wear traditional, regional dress.

along the way. The bride rides in the last wagon, which is covered with flowers.

The reception is usually held at the bride's parents' house. There, the bride's wreath is taken off and her hair is unbraided to show that she is now a wife. Before anyone else can dance, the bride must dance with every man there, and finally with her new husband.

When the party ends, the bride goes around her

parents' house saying good-bye to the rooms, furniture, and kitchen utensils that were part of her life there. At their new home, the bride and groom look up the chimney. According to tradition, this ensures that the devil is not hiding inside! They also walk around the dining table three times for good luck. A new Polish family has begun.

Family Ties

Poles have a strong sense of family. In past generations, families were often large. A person might have five or seven or even ten brothers and sisters, especially if the family had a lot of farm work to do. As more and more people moved to cities and worked in factories, families grew smaller.

Most Polish children today have only one or two brothers and sisters, or are only children. But to a Pole, family means more than just parents and children. Grandparents, uncles, aunts, cousins, and more distant relatives are all included. Poles also like to "adopt" good friends who seem as close as family. Every possible family member and friend is usually invited to important family occasions, such as weddings or funerals. People often come from long distances for these events.

Family ties remain strong when people emigrate to other countries. Many Poles in the United States, Canada, and around the world regularly send letters, presents, and money to relatives in Poland—sometimes even to relatives they have never met. Anytime one of these "foreign" relatives comes to Poland, a royal welcome is guaranteed.

The Housing Shortage

Poles welcome guests into their homes even though they have much less space and money than most Americans do. A shortage of housing is one of Poland's greatest problems. So many houses were destroyed during World War II that, even now, there is not enough housing for everyone.

People often share rooms with other family members. A family of four might have two large rooms, a bathroom, and a small kitchen. Grandparents sometimes live with their children and grandchildren. When a couple gets married, they may have to live with the bride's or groom's parents for several years while they are waiting for their own apartment to be built.

It can take five years or even longer between the time a Pole signs up for a new apartment and the time it is ready to be lived in. The government builds some apartments, and these are the least expensive. Apartments are also built by private groups called construction cooperatives. They are often a group of people from the same factory, profession, or trade group.

Although Poles do not have as much space as most

Traditional Polish architecture.

North Americans do, and must wait a long time for a new home, they do not have to spend as large a part of their income on housing. In North America, many people pay one-third of their income for a home. In Poland, housing used to cost as little as seven percent of the family's earnings. As Poland has moved toward a market economy, housing costs for many have risen dramatically.

In almost every Polish family, both parents work full-time at a factory, office, or on a farm. Most adults work six days a week, Monday through Saturday. Though Poles must work longer hours than North Americans, in some ways they have better working conditions. Vacations are longer—at least a month for most workers.

Women in Poland

The constitution formed by the Communist government in 1945 guarantees that men and women are equal and are entitled to equal pay and employment. Both men and women can be found doing nearly every kind of work. Polish women do say, however, that it is more difficult for them than for men to get the very highest positions in most factories or offices.

Poland has an excellent day care system. While parents work, children who are too young to go to school often stay in nurseries. Some factories and offices have their own day care for the children of the people who work there. Many young children, though, stay with their grandparents during the day instead.

Maternity benefits are better in Poland than in America, too. A new mother can stay at home with her baby for four months with pay. If she chooses, she can also take a leave of absence for three years. A leave of absence means that she will not lose her job, but will not be paid while she is at home.

Like North American families, Polish ones differ in the way they take care of household chores. As in North America, some mothers complain that they really have two jobs: their paid job, plus the unpaid job of doing all the housework. In other families, fathers, children, and grandparents also do a lot of the cooking, cleaning, and other chores.

Smacznego!

Polish meals are different than North American ones. Poles start the day with breakfast before they go to school or work. But unlike North Americans, Poles do not have lunch at work. Instead, they eat a second breakfast at ten or eleven in the morning, often at their work desks, or during a break between classes at school.

The biggest meal of the Polish day, *obiad*, is like an American dinner. Poles serve soup, meat or fish, potatoes, vegetables, and dessert for obiad. Obiad is usually eaten

A man eats ice cream by a line of people waiting to buy the same thing.

after work, between three and five o'clock. Later in the evening, at about eight or nine, they eat their last light meal.

In Poland it would be unusual to eat a steak or hamburger. Like many Europeans, Poles eat more veal and pork than beef. They do not like to drink plain water when they can have tea, beer, vodka, or fruit juice instead, and they don't usually use ice cubes in their drinks. Since oranges and other citrus fruits do not grow in Poland, they are very expensive. An orange or a grapefruit is a special treat that can be bought only a few months of the year.

Instead of expensive imported fruits and vegetables, Poles usually eat the ones that grow on Polish farms. Potatoes, beets, cabbage, spinach, apples, pears, currants, and strawberries are some of the fresh vegetables and fruits Poles grow themselves.

Poles are known for their soups—made from a variety of vegetables and meats, with a broth or milk base. *Barszcz* is made with beets, and *kapusniak* is sauerkraut soup. There are many kinds of fruit soups, too, such as *czarnina*, made with duck and prunes.

Some Polish foods are not familiar to Americans. *Pierogi*, for example, are envelopes of dough that can be stuffed with meat, sauerkraut, fresh cabbage, a mixture of potatoes and cheese, or fruits. They can be served as a main dish, side dish, or dessert. *Naleszniki*, thin pancakes, can also be stuffed with many different fillings. And *Bigos*, hunter's stew, is a tasty mixture of sausage, sauerkraut, fresh cabbage, pork, and spices that is cooked slowly for hours.

There are plenty of delicious Polish cakes, too. Some are only a bit sweet: poppyseed cake, cake stuffed with cream cheese filling, and some fruit cakes, for example. Honey cakes, gingerbread, rum cake, and *paczki*—ball-shaped doughnuts filled with jelly and rolled in sugar—are all much sweeter. A *mazurek* or *placek*, small cakes, may also have sweet icing or be made with different kinds of fruit or jam.

A Polish Meal

Here is a traditional and tasty Polish meal to make for your family and friends!

Red Cabbage and Apple Salad

4 cups red cabbage, grated
salt
2 apples
2 onions, diced
sugar
pepper
salad oil

☛Put the grated cabbage on a plate and sprinkle it with salt to soften the cabbage. ☛Grate the apple, using a grater with big holes. ☛When the cabbage is soft, mix it with the grated apple and onion. ☛ Sprinkle with a pinch of sugar, a little pepper, and a little salad oil.

Bigos

1 pound boneless pork
7 or 8 ounces of Polish sausage (kielbasa), sliced
2 ounces of bacon
4 cups sauerkraut, largely chopped
1/2 head of cabbage, shredded

1 medium onion, chopped
3 dried mushrooms, chopped
2 cloves garlic, mashed
5 tablespoons tomato preserves
2 tablespoons of flour
cooking oil
bay leaf
allspice
salt

☛In a large pot, cover sauerkraut with water. Simmer for 15 to 20 minutes. ☛In a second pot, cover cabbage, mushrooms, and garlic with water. Simmer for 20 to 25 minutes. ☛Cut boneless pork into cubes. Sprinkle with salt. Brown in frying pan with a small amount of oil. ☛Fry bacon on low heat. ☛Add bacon, pork, bay leaf, and a sprinkling of allspice to sauerkraut mixture.

☛After sauerkraut mixture has cooked for 15 to 20 minutes add sausage and cooked cabbage. ☛Brown onion in oil. ☛Add flour and stir. Add to bigos. ☛Simmer bigos on low heat for at least an hour. Stir occasionally. Add water as needed, but bigos should be thick. ☛Serve with fresh Polish rye bread and butter.

This recipe serves four to six people. But, many people think that bigos tastes even better when reheated after a day or two, so don't worry if there are leftovers!

Fried Apple Dessert

2 eggs
2 cups flour
2/3 cup water
6 large green apples, cored
2 teaspoons butter or cooking oil
powdered sugar

☛Mix eggs, flour, and water. Set batter aside. ☛Slice the apples into pieces about 1/3-inch thick. ☛Heat the butter or cooking oil in a large frying pan until it sizzles. ☛Dip each slice into the batter, and put it in the pan. When it looks brown, turn it over. ☛When the apples are brown on both sides, drop them into a bowl of powdered sugar, covering both sides. ☛Eat them right away—but don't burn your tongue!

Before you start eating the Polish meal, wish each other *"Smacznego!"* That's what Poles say at the beginning of a meal. It means "I hope your food is delicious, and you enjoy your meal!"

8. Education, Polish Style

School is important in the lives of Polish children, just as it is in the United States and most other countries. In some ways, Polish schools are much like schools in North America. Students take classes, look forward to seeing their friends, and have homework.

However, like other European schools, Polish schools are much more challenging than most North American schools. Students take more subjects, study difficult subjects at earlier ages, and have more homework. For example, Polish students in sixth grade often take algebra, which most Americans don't begin until high school. All Polish students begin a foreign language in elementary school, with Russian, German, and English being the most common. Polish students have studied at least one, and very often two, for six to ten years before college.

A Lot to Learn

Polish students go to school six days a week, Monday through Saturday, although they have fewer school hours each day than Americans do. School usually starts at eight or nine in the morning and ends by one or two in the afternoon. Students have some subjects every day, such

Music class at a public grammar school.

as Polish or mathematics. Other subjects, such as art or gym, may meet two or three times a week. Because of this, students do not have the same schedule every day.

Polish elementary schools start with kindergarten and go through eighth grade. In the first few grades, schoolchildren have the same teacher all day. But starting in the fourth or fifth grade, there is a different teacher for each subject. The students stay in the same classrooms all day, and the teachers go from room to room.

When they start school, they learn how to read and write in Polish. They also learn math, Polish history, world history, geography, biology, chemistry, and physics. In addition, they study art and music, and learn about Polish and foreign literature. Other elementary school subjects are citizenship, health, cooking, and crafts. Usually a student takes five or more subjects at once, and older children study more subjects than younger students.

School Rules

Polish schoolchildren are expected to follow strict rules. In many schools, when they arrive in the morning, they leave their shoes with their coats in the cloakroom. Then they put on slippers to keep the floors clean. Many Polish students also put on school smocks. The smocks have badges on them with the school's name and number. All students have numbers, too, and often they are called on by number instead of by name.

Each student shares a big desk with another student. Schoolchildren all have a special notebook for each class in which they write all their notes and homework for that subject for the whole year. They often have jobs, such as cleaning blackboards, to help take care of the school. When the teacher comes into the room, students are expected to stand up and politely say hello.

During class, a Polish school would probably seem more formal than an American one. But between classes, students have more freedom. They have a short break after each class, and one or two longer breaks during the day when they can go out and play. Even during the short breaks, they do not have to stay in the school building. They play, chat, and talk about school. Sometimes they bring food from home or go get some *lody* (ice cream) or *woda sodowa* (soda) from a vendor's cart on the street corner.

After School

Even though Polish students can go home early in the afternoon when classes are finished, they often stay later. Since both mothers and fathers usually work all day, it might be four or five o'clock before parents come home. Many young people stay late to go to music lessons, join club activities, play sports, or learn crafts. There are also special classes for students who want to do their own chemistry experiments, study Polish poetry, or learn English.

Sometimes the older students are getting ready for a school's "Olympics." This is an academic contest in which they compete against students from other schools in different subjects. Doing well in the Olympics can help a student get into a better high school.

Polish students often take field trips with their classes. Sometimes they go to a museum or to a movie. They often

A young boy during his cello lesson.

go to places that are important in Polish history: castles, battlefields, or the house where Chopin was born, for example. At other times, they go into the woods for nature trips. In the north, students take trips to the beach by the Baltic Sea. In the south, where there are mountains, they go hiking and camping. Some field trips are short—just an hour or two to a nearby park or important building. But other trips last all day, or even for two or three days.

Higher Education

Every child in Poland must finish elementary school. But after students graduate from eighth grade, there are several different things they might do. Some children, especially farm children, start working after graduation. Most, though, go on to another school.

Many students go to a vocational school—a school that teaches them how to do a job. In a vocational school, students study for about three years. They can learn how to do many kinds of jobs in factories and businesses. When they graduate, they go to work.

Other students, especially those who want to go to college, go to high school for four or five years. There are two different kinds of high schools in Poland. One kind is for people who are interested in technical careers. These students might want to be agricultural scientists, industrial engineers, or computer designers, for example.

Some of them go to work after high school, but others go on to a technical college in their field.

The other kind of high school is for students interested in the liberal arts—languages, literature, art and music, and some sciences. These students usually go on to a university after they graduate. They might want to be teachers, art historians, or astronomers.

The choice of a secondary school (vocational or high school) depends partly on the student's career plans, and partly on his or her performance in elementary school. Students from cities can usually find the kind of vocational or high school they want in their home towns. But some students, especially those from rural areas, must travel to school. Sometimes they take a bus or train back and forth every day. If their home is far enough away from a big school, students live in a dormitory, a building they share with other students on campus.

The advantage to the Polish system of secondary education is that it gives much more specific preparation for the student's future career or college studies than American schools do. The disadvantage is that not everyone is ready to make major decisions about his or her education or career plans at the end of eighth grade. It's more difficult for a Pole (or other European) to decide on a college education if he or she is in vocational school than it is for an American in a general high school.

Every high school senior who wants to go on to

Warsaw University.

college must take a test called the *matura*, which is given nationwide once a year. The colleges know the grades of everyone who took the test that year. Then they choose the best students for each field of study.

Under the Communist system, the government decided exactly how many new workers would be needed in each field. If there were 550 jobs for geographers, for example, only 550 students would be chosen to study geography. As market forces become more important in the Polish economy, the numbers will probably not be quite so exact. Still, universities in both Eastern and

Western Europe limit the numbers of openings more than North American ones do.

For the students, this system has both good and bad sides. A Polish college graduate knows that he or she will probably get a job in the right field. Students do not have to pay for college. In fact, they often get extra money from the college as well as free room and board.

However, this system also means that there is a lot of pressure to earn a high grade on the matura. It can determine the entire future of students. They study for months ahead of time. If they don't get a high enough grade to get into college the first time, they have to wait for a year to take the test again.

Young people aren't the only ones who go to school in Poland. Just as in North America, adults often take evening courses. Some do this to get better jobs, or help their performance at work, but many take courses just for the fun of it. Most Poles of all ages consider education very important—something that requires hard work, but can make life better.

9. *Sports and Fun for Everyone*

Like all people, Poles find many ways to enjoy themselves. Polish boys and girls like to play many of the same games Americans do—volleyball and basketball, for example. But the most popular team sport is soccer. Soccer, which is called "football" in Europe, is as popular in Poland as American football is in the United States.

When an important soccer tournament such as the World Cup is being played, there may be 800 million people around the world watching it on TV. Since only about half of the Polish homes have television sets, many people visit their friends to watch an important game if they don't have one themselves. When a Polish team is doing well—everyone cheers and some people have parties. In 1974, when the Polish team played in the World Cup finals, Poles were very excited. There are many Polish soccer teams, but a team called Gornik Zabrze has been the number one team for years.

Sports For Fun

Polish boys and girls play soccer, basketball, and volleyball at school. Many play just for fun at recess, and some children play on school teams. Teams from different schools often play against each other. Adults play, too, on factory or office teams.

Individual sports are also very popular in Poland. In cities and towns there are public gymnasiums, indoor and outdoor swimming pools, and ice skating rinks as well as volleyball courts and soccer fields. People can use these sports centers for free, or for a very small fee.

Poles who are interested in a sport can join a sports union that belongs to the national Society for the Promotion of Physical Culture. In the sports unions, people make friends while enjoying soccer, volleyball, swimming, sailing, or other sports. The Polish government also has a recreation department that offers activities for travelers, both foreign visitors and Poles. The department and the sports unions also have classes for people who want to learn a sport, and hold local and national contests throughout the year.

Poland is a good place for winter sports as well as summer ones. Skiing is very popular, especially in the southern mountains. People who like to ski come from other parts of Poland or from other countries for a vacation in Zakopane or another mountain town. Children often join skiing clubs at school.

Children in all parts of Poland also like to sled and ice skate. Sometimes they bring sleds or skates to school so they can use them at recess. Some schools even make their own skating rinks in the winter.

The Champions

Most Poles play games and sports just to enjoy them. But a few young people who are especially good at a sport join the Olympic teams or other national teams.

The Polish soccer team won the gold medal at the 1972 Olympics in Munich, and the silver medal in 1976 at Montreal. The volleyball team captured the gold in Montreal.

In addition to their soccer and volleyball victories, Poles win prizes in individual sports. In the 1988 Olympics, two Polish men won gold medals, one in judo and one in wrestling. Polish men and women have also won medals in track and field events. One gold medal winner at the 1980 Olympics in Moscow was Wladyslaw Kozakiewicz. Leaping higher than anyone had ever done before, he set a new record for the pole vault. The first woman to run one hundred yards in less than eleven seconds was a Pole, Stella Walsh. She was a star sprinter in the 1930s and won gold medals in the 1932 and 1936 Olympics. In 1980, another Polish woman, Grazyna Rabsztyn, beat women from around the world to set a world record in the one-hundred-meter hurdles.

Poles have also broken world records in weight-lifting, target shooting, and skiing. Ski jumper Wojciech Fortuna and slalom skier Andrzej Bachleda are known by skiing fans throughout the world.

A young gymnast hovers above the crowd during a sports demonstration.

Throughout history, many strong Polish men have found fame in weight-lifting, boxing, and wrestling. In fact, a man many sports historians call one of the five best wrestlers of all time was a Pole. His real name was Stanislaw Cyganiewicz, but he was known as "Zbysko."

Zbysko lived from 1881 to 1967, and won contests against much younger men when he was in his forties and fifties. He was not just an athlete, either. He knew eleven languages and was a poet, musician, and a lawyer as well as a wrestler. He also invented a tilt-top exercise table, and received a patent for it in 1964.

More recently, Krystyna Chojnowska Liskiewicz sailed her thirty-two foot (10-meter) sailboat, *Mazurek*, around the world. She was the first woman ever to make this voyage alone and she had several mishaps. She had to stop sailing and spend three weeks in the hospital at one point. While near the Panama Canal, she was almost run over by a freighter. Once, while she was on shore, her boat drifted away and was almost lost. However, two years and twenty-four days after she began in March of 1976, she completed her journey.

Vacation Time

Most Poles do not take round-the-world trips, but they do like to travel within Poland. With the changes in Poland and the rest of Eastern Europe, travel to other countries has become a great deal easier. However, foreign travel is still too expensive for most Poles to afford.

But within Poland, even the longest trips take only a day or two. That makes it easy for Polish families or school groups to take weekend trips to see other parts of Poland. And, since most Polish workers have about four weeks of vacation time, families can take long vacations together. Poles who work in factories can often take a free vacation paid for by the factory where they work.

Poles often vacation in cities where they can see historic buildings and go to concerts, theaters, and museums. Each Polish city has its own history and its own special places to explore. Some special festivals are held, such as the Warsaw Autumn, where modern music is played every summer. These festivals attract people from all over the world.

Poles also like to go to the country for vacations. There are many different kinds of countryside for people with different interests—mountains, lakes, the seacoast, forests, and even a small desert not far from Krakow. The mountains are good places for hiking and for raft rides on mountain streams in summertime. In the northeast there are large forests much like the ones that covered all of Europe centuries ago.

The Bialowieska Forest is one of the oldest. Much of it is preserved in a national park. About one hundred European bison live there. This is the largest herd in the

Poles ride bicycles everywhere. These children take a break on a park bench in Wadowice, birthplace of the Pope.

world of these rare animals, which look like North American buffaloes.

Along the northern coast are the many beaches by the Baltic Sea where summer visitors come to swim and sunbathe. Sometimes people take boat trips to small islands not far from the coast. One popular island is named Hel. English-speaking visitors send postcards from this island with messages such as, "I went to Hel today and had a devil of a time!"

The Mazurian lakes in the northeast, and the Pomeranian lakes farther west, are very popular places for vacations, too. Here, there are thousands of small lakes in slightly rolling forest land. Many are connected by rivers, streams, or canals. People like to go sailing, fishing, or canoeing on these lakes. Vacationers like to stay by the lakes, either in tents, cottages, or country hotels.

Whether they are at home or on vacation, Poles like to walk, hike, and ride bicycles. Children often take short hiking or cycling trips with their friends or families.

Poland is full of interesting places to explore. Even without going far from home, Polish young people may have castles, parks, forests, lakes, and ancient streets to see in their own home towns. Their country is truly a place that has sports and fun for everyone.

10. A Home Away from Home

In the 1500s, news of a "New World" in America was spreading through Europe. Some of the earliest books with stories and maps of the Americas were printed in Poland. In fact, some people say that Jan Kolmar, a Pole who was captain of a Danish ship, reached Canada sixteen years before Columbus' first voyage in 1492. Whether that is truth or legend, Polish settlers did arrive at the English colony of Jamestown in 1608. The Poles built a glassworks there, which may have been the first American factory. They also held the first strike, because the English would not let the Poles vote on Jamestown's laws.

A Good Cause

Only a few Poles emigrated before the mid-1700s. But the American Revolution appealed to Poles who wanted the same democratic rights in Poland. Some of them came to help the American rebels fight Britain. Count Casimir Pulaski, who organized the U.S. cavalry, and Haym Solomon, who lent the new U.S. government money it needed to fight the war, came from Poland in the 1700s. Both of them had been ordered to leave Poland because they opposed the Polish king. Pulaski stayed in America, where he died of a battle wound.

Probably the most well known Pole who helped American forces was Tadeusz Kosciuszko. This skilled engineer designed many U.S. forts and bridges. Kosciuszko proved his belief in human rights time and time again. During the hard winters of the Revolutionary War, he spent his own money to make sure that the British prisoners in American camps had enough to eat. He also opposed slavery long before most Americans did. He left money in his will to buy and free slaves, and used money from land sales to start one of the first schools for African Americans.

Kosciuszko took his knowledge of revolution and returned to Poland. There he led the 1794 uprising against Russia after the partitions of Poland. The Poles lost, and Kosciuszko again had to live in other countries after he was freed from a Russian prison.

After each of the partitions of Poland, Poles emigrated in greater numbers. Often they had to leave for political reasons. After the unsuccessful fights for Polish freedom in 1794, 1830-1831, 1848, and 1883, several thousand Poles left for other countries. Most of these people were well educated. Many were aristocrats, people of noble birth.

Economic reasons also caused many Poles to leave their homeland. During the troubled 1800s, some landowners lost their land because of debts or anti-Polish laws. In farm families, there were often so many children that the tradition of dividing the family farm among them would have been impossible. Also, there were years, especially in the 1870s, when crops failed and Poles did not have enough to eat. As a result, some Poles went to other countries to find farm and factory work until they had enough money to return to Poland. Others decided to go to a country where it would be easier to buy land.

Many Workers, Many Jobs

The United States was a popular place to go for new farmland because so much of it was available at such low prices. Poles established farming communities in Wisconsin, Minnesota, North and South Dakota, and other states. Polish farmers also settled in the Canadian provinces of Ontario and Manitoba, and in several South American countries—especially Brazil.

After 1870, Polish immigration to America increased greatly. In Poland, crops were failing and unemployment was rising. In the United States, the Civil War was over, and many industries were growing fast. Factories of many kinds needed both skilled and unskilled workers. Millions of Europeans came to America between 1870 and 1914. After 1900, Poles were usually one of the four largest groups of incoming immigrants each year.

A Polish-American coal miner after a hard day's work in a Pennsylvania mine.

Many Polish men found jobs in coal mines and the iron and steel industries because they had worked in these industries in Poland. Polish communities in many Pennsylvanian cities and towns, and in such places as Buffalo, New York, and Chicago's southeast side, were founded by these workers.

Polish men and women also worked in many other industries. Life was hard for factory workers in the late 1800s. They often had to work ten to twelve hours a day at hard, tiring jobs which paid only two to five dollars a week. Even though food, housing, and other things cost much less than they do now, those wages were barely enough to live on. Like other immigrant laborers, Poles often had to live in crowded tenements and did not always have enough to eat.

Not all Polish immigrants were unskilled workers. Some knew a trade and held skilled jobs as cabinet makers, carpenters, blacksmiths, printers, dressmakers, tailors, and jewelers.

Other Polish Americans who had saved enough money in city jobs usually bought houses or apartment buildings as soon as they could afford them. Many bought neighborhood stores and saloons—especially in Polish neighborhoods. Often everyone in the family worked in these small businesses.

After 1900, there were more doctors, dentists, engineers, teachers, professors, musicians, actors, and artists in the Polish community. Some of these were new immigrants, while others were second generation Poles.

Difficult Years

The years just before World War I were a difficult time for Poles who wanted to keep their traditional language and customs in America. New immigrants from Poland made the Polish-American communities (usually called *Polonia*) larger and stronger each year. However, this was a time when some native-born Americans feared or hated people from other countries. They tried to make Poles and other immigrants stop using their native languages and keeping their native customs. Polish children were sometimes teased or punished in school for speaking Polish. Adults sometimes had to pass English tests for jobs where knowing English was not needed to do the work.

During the early 1900s, officials of the American Roman Catholic church—most of whom were Irish Americans—tried to keep Polish communities from using Polish in their churches and church schools. They also refused to appoint Polish Americans to high church positions. These actions made many Polish-American Catholics so angry that some of their churches broke away and formed the Polish National Catholic church. This action caused the church leaders to allow them to keep using Polish as well as English in the remaining churches.

During World War I, from 1914 to 1918, there was less emigration from Poland because it was hard for people to leave Europe. Polish Americans gave money and political support to the movement for an independent Poland. The Polish pianist Ignacy Paderewski was the leader of this movement. He gave speeches and concerts throughout America, and talked to President Woodrow Wilson and other government leaders.

Polish Americans were overjoyed when a new Polish nation was formed at the conclusion of World War I. About 75,000 of them joined Poles from all over the world in returning to Poland to help build the new nation.

But the new Poland had severe economic problems, including unemployment. As a result, some Poles also came to the United States during the 1920s and 1930s to find jobs. Coming to America was not as easy as it had been before World War I. In 1921, the U.S. government passed a new, strict immigration law which restricted the numbers of immigrants from some parts of the world—especially Asia, southern Europe, and central Europe.

War and Postwar Life

September 1939 was a time of great sadness for Polish Americans because of the German and Russian invasion of Poland. World War II came so suddenly that some Poles who thought they were just making a short visit to the United States became immigrants. Among them were painter Eliasz Kanarek and math professor Stanislaw Ulam. Ulam later served on the scientific team that developed the atomic bomb during World War II. Two famous musicians, harpsichordist Wanda Landowska and pianist Artur Rubinstein, also came to escape the Nazis.

After World War II, many of the Poles who had supported non-Communist political groups sought refuge in the United States. Some of them were officials of the former Polish government.

During the 1960s, 1970s, and 1980s, many Poles traveled to America to find better paying jobs or for political reasons. After martial law was declared in 1981, for example, some Solidarity members left Poland for the United States.

Today, the United States has more people of Polish descent than any other country but Poland. Depending on how many generations are counted, there are from 7 to 15 million Poles in America. There are also more than 324,000 Poles in Canada.

In the United States, Chicago's Polonia is by far the largest. Counting both city and suburbs, Chicago has close to one million Poles—more than any city in the world except Warsaw. Buffalo, Detroit, Milwaukee,

Cleveland, Pittsburgh, Philadelphia, and New York also have large Polish communities. Some smaller cities also have large Polish populations. These include South Bend, Indiana, Scranton, Pennsylvania, and Youngstown, Ohio.

Life in Polonia

In the larger Polonias, it is easy to find streets where people speak Polish or see shops that have signs in both Polish and English. Churches in these neighborhoods have Polish mass on Sunday, bless Easter baskets, and give out the oplatek at Christmas.

Not all third- or fourth-generation Polish Americans keep traditional ways or are interested in Poland. But many of them do care about their Polish backgrounds. Since the 1970s, especially, many Polish Americans have been joining Polish organizations—even if their parents and grandparents were not active in Polonia.

There are more than ten thousand Polish-American organizations in the United States. There are clubs for Polish dentists, Polish scout troops, and organizations to preserve Polish art and music—just about any kind of club you can imagine!

Some of these organizations are small, local groups, but others are large national groups. The largest Polish-American organization is the Polish National Alliance (PNA). This fraternal insurance company has more than

A cultural and ethnic parade for Polish Americans in Chicago. The city has more people of Polish descent than any other except Warsaw.

325,000 members. Other national organizations include the Polish Roman Catholic Union, the Polish-American Congress, the Polish Women's Alliance, the Polish Falcons, and the American Council of Polish Culture.

Polish Americans also have many radio shows, several daily newspapers, and even a few television shows. Many newsletters and magazines are published by different groups. Some shows and publications are in Polish, some in English, and some in both languages.

Civil Rights and Politics

Polish Americans have played major parts in the fight for freedom within America. Before the Civil War, many were active in the movement to end slavery. One of these abolitionists, Ernestine Potowski-Rose, also played a key role in persuading the New York State legislature to pass an important women's rights law in 1848. This was the first U.S. law that gave married women as much right to own land and take care of their children as married men had. Before, children had legally belonged only to their fathers, and wives had to have their husbands' permission to own land.

Also in the mid-1800s, Dr. Elzbieta Zakrzewska, one of the first female doctors, founded two hospitals where female doctors could learn and work. Before, even if a woman graduated from a medical school, she might not have found a job. Most hospitals did not want to hire female doctors.

Polish Americans are still involved in shaping the lives and laws of the United States. Polish Americans have been mayors and government officials in many large cities. They have also served in the U.S. Congress. Current Polish Americans in Congress include Daniel Rostenkowski of Illinois, the chairperson of the House Ways and Means Committee; Barbara Mikulski, a senator from Maryland; and Alaskan Senator Frank Murkowski.

Illinois Congressman Daniel Rostenkowski, Chairman of both the Committee on Ways and Means and the Joint Committee on Taxation.

Edmund Muskie, a former senator and governor of Maine, ran for vice-president in 1968, and served as secretary of state in 1980. Zbigniew Brzezinski has been an important political advisor on Soviet affairs and national security, first to President Lyndon Johnson and later to President Jimmy Carter. Under President George Bush, Edward Derwinski is secretary of Veterans' Affairs.

Arts and Sports

Poland has given the United States several of its best symphony conductors—Leopold Stokowski, Artur Rodzinski, and Stanislaw Skrowaczewski, in addition to many opera singers, pianists, and string players. The music in quite a few American movies was written by a Pole, Bronislaw Kaper.

Other Poles have made contributions to American movies and television. One of the first well-known actresses in silent films was Pola Negri. Modern TV stars have included Loretta Swit (Hotlips on "M*A*S*H") and Ted Knight (Ted Baxter on "The Mary Tyler Moore Show").

Poles have been important behind the scenes, too. The Warner brothers—two born in Poland, one in Canada —founded one of Hollywood's biggest film studios. Joseph Tycociner invented movie film that has sound.

Many American soccer players are of Polish descent

and Polish Americans have made notable contributions to baseball and football. At least one Polish-American college football star has won All American honors nearly every year since 1927. Stan Musial, Carl Yastrzembski, and Gene Malinowski are familiar names to fans of professional sports. Steve Gromek and Stan Lopata are current professional athletes. Bob Milacki of the Baltimore Orioles was baseball's 1989 rookie of the year.

Everyday Polish-Americans

Of course, it isn't only the famous Poles who have contributed to the United States. Ordinary Poles have also helped by working hard, settling new land, making city neighborhoods clean and safe, building beautiful churches, serving in the armed forces. They have also brought Polish art and music to a new land as well as their own ideas about freedom and individual rights.

Like children who love both their parents, Poles who have settled in the United States and elsewhere are able to love their new lands without forgetting their love for Poland. After all, the Polish national anthem begins with the words, *"Jeszce Polska nie zginela—Poki my zyjemy"*—"Poland will never die as long as we are alive." No matter where they go, that's a song Poles like to remember.

Appendix A
Polish Embassies and Consulates in the United States and Canada

The Polish consulates in the United States and Canada offer assistance and information about all aspects of Polish life. For more information and resource materials, contact the embassy or consulate nearest you.

U.S. Consulates and Embassy

Chicago, Illinois
Consulate General of Poland
1530 N. Lake Shore Drive
Chicago, Illinois 60610
Phone (312) 237-8166

New York, New York
Polish Consulate General
233 N. Madison Avenue
New York, New York 10016
Phone (212) 889-8360

Washington, D.C.
Embassy of the Republic of Poland
2640 16th Street, N.W.
Washington, D.C. 20008

Consular Division of the Polish Embassy
2244 Wyoming Avenue, N.W.
Washington, D.C.
Phone for both (202) 234-3800

Canadian Consulates and Embassy

Montreal, Quebec
Consulate General of Poland
1500 Pine Avenue, W.
Montreal, Quebec H3G 1B4
Phone (514) 937-9481

Ottawa, Ontario
Embassy of Poland
433 Daly Avenue
Ottawa, Ontario K1N 6H3
Phone (613) 236-0468

Toronto, Ontario
Consulate General of Poland
2603 Lakeshore Boulevard, W.
Toronto Ontario M8V 1G
Phone (416) 252-8747

Appendix B
Pronunciation Guide of Polish People and Places*

PEOPLE
August, Zygmunt (ZIHG-moont)
Bachleda, Andrzej (bahk-LEH-duh, AHND-jay)
Brzezinski, Zbigniew (bzhuh-ZEEN-skee, zBEEG-nyehv)
Chopin, Fryderyk (SHAW-pan, frih-duh-rihk)
Curie, Maria Sklodowska (KYUH-ree, MAH-ree-uh skwuh-DUHF-skuh)
Cyganiewicz, Stanislaw (tsih-gah-NYEH-veech, stah-NEES-wahf)
***Derwinski, Edward**
Dubrawa (duh-BRAH-vuh)
Fortuna, Wojciech (for-TOO-nuh, VOY-chehk)
Funk, Kazimierz (FUNK, ka-ZHEE-myehzh)
Gierek, Edward (GYEH-rehk, ed-vahrd)
Gomulka, Wladyslaw (guh-MOOW-kuh, vwah-DEES-wahv)
***Gromek, Steve**
Grotowski, Jerzy (groh-TOV-skee, YEH-zuh)
Hilderica (heel-duh-REE-kuh)
Jadwiga(jahd-VEE-guh)
Jagiello (jahg-YEH-waw)
Janosik (yah-NAW-sheek)
Jaruzelski, Wojciech (yah-roo-ZEHL-skee, VOY-chek)
Kanarek, Eliasz (kah-NAH-rek, EHL-ee-ahsh)
Kaper, Bronislaw (KAH-pehr, brah-NEE-swahf)
Kazimierz (kah-ZHEE-myehzh) **the Great**
Kinga (KING-uh)
Kochanowski, Jan (kaw-kaw-NAHF-skee, YAHN)
Kolmar, Jan (KAWL-mahr, YAHN)
Kopernik, Mikolaj (kaw-PEHR-neek, MEE-KAW-weye)
Korzeniowski, Josef Konrad (kaw-zhe-NEE-AWF-skee, YAH-zef-KAHN-rahd)

---

* No pronunciation is given for names that have been Anglicized.

Kosciuszko, Tadeusz (kaws-CHEE-OOS-kaw, tah-DEH-us)
Kozakiewicz, Wladyslaw (kah-zah-KYEH-vihtch, vwah-DEES-wahf)
Krak (KRAHK)
Landowska, Wanda (lahn-DAHF-skuh, VAHN-duh)
Liskiewicz, Krystyna Chojnowska (lees-KYEH-veech, krihs-TIH-nah hoy-
    NUHF-skah)
*Lopata, Stan
Lukasziewicz, Ignacy (loo-kuh-SHEH-veech, ihg-NAH-tsee)
Lutoslawski, Witold (loo-tuh-SWAHF-skee, VEE-tohld)
*Malinowski, Gene
Mazowiecki, Tadeusz (ma-zuh-VYEHS-kee, tah-DEH-us)
Mieszko (MYEHSH-kaw)
*Mikulski, Barbara
Milosz, Czeslaw (MEE-wawsh, CHEHS-wahf)
Modjeska, Helena (mawd-JEHS-kuh, heh-leh-nuh)
Moniuszko, Stanislaw (muh-NYOOS-kaw, stah-NEES-wahf)
*Murkowski, Frank
*Muskie, Edmund
Negri, Pola (NEH-gree, PAW-lah)
Orszula (awr-SHOO-luh)
Paderewski, Ignacy (pah-deh-REHF-skee, eeg-NAHT-see)
Penderecki, Krzystof (pehn-deh-REHT-skee, KZHIHS-tawf)
Piast (PYAHST)
Pilsudski, Jozef (peel-SOOD-skee, YOO-sehf)
Poniatowski, Stanislaw (pawn-yuh-TAWF-skee, stah-NEES-wahf)
Popiel (PAW-pyehl)
Potowski-Rose, Ernestine (pah-TAWF-skee-ROZ, EHR-nuh-steen)
Pulaski, Kazimierz (poo-WAH-skee, kah-ZHEE-myezh)
Rabsztyn, Grazyna (RAHB-shtihn, grah-ZHEE-nuh)
Reymont, Wladyslaw (RAY-mahnt, vwah-DIHS-wahf)
Rodzinski, Artur (rawd-ZHEEN-skee, AHR-toor)
*Rostenkowski, Daniel
Rubinstein, Artur (ROO-bihn-steyen, AHR-toor)

Sienkiewicz, Henryk (shee-ehn-KEE-EH-veech, HEHN-rihk)
Skrowaczewski, Stanislaw (skroh-vuh-CHEHF-skee, stan-NEES-wahf)
Sobieski, Jan (soh-BYEH-skee, YAHN)
Solomon, Haym (SAHL-uh-muhn, HEYEM)
Stokowski, Leopold (staw-KAWF-skee, LEH-aw-pawld)
Szymanowski, Karol (shih-muh-NOHF-skee, KAH-rohl)
Tomaszewski, Henryk (taw-muh-SHEHF-skee, HEHN-rihk)
Twardowski, Pan (twahr-DAWF-skee, PAHN)
Ulam, Stanislaw (OO-lahm, stah-NEE-swahf)
Wajda, Andrzej (VEYE-duh, AHND-jay)
Walesa, Lech (vuh-WEHN-suh, LEHK)
Walsh, Stella (VAHLSH, STEHL-luh)
Wladyslaw (vwah-DIHS-wahf) **the Short**
Wojtyla, Karol (voy-TIH-wuh, KAH-rawl)
Wyszynski, Stefan (vih-SHIHN-skee, STEH-fahn)
*Yastrzembski, Carl
Zakrzewska, Elzbieta (zahk-ZHEHF-skah, ehlzh-BEE-EH-tuh)
Zbysko (z-BIHS-kaw)

PLACES
*Baltic Sea
Bialowieska (bee-yah-wuh-VEEYEHS-kuh)
Biskupin (bee-SKOO-peen)
Bug (BOOG) **River**
*Carpathian Mountains
Czestochowa (chow-staw-HOH-vuh)
Galicia (guh-LEE-tsee-uh)
Gdansk (gdeyensk)
Gdynia (GDIHN-yuh)
Gniezno (GNYEE-ehzh-nah)
Goplo, Lake (GOHP-wuh)
Hel (hehl)
Jagiellonian (jahg-yeh-LOH-nee-uhm) **University**
Jasna Gora (YAHZ-nuh GOO-ruh)

Kasubia (kah-SHOO-bee-uh)
Katowice (kah-toh-WEE-tsuh)
Krakow (KRAHK-oof)
Lodz (WOODSH)
Lowicz (WUH-veech)
Malopolska (mah-wah-POHL-skuh)
Mariacki (mah-ree-AHCH-kee)
Mazowsze (muh-ZAHF-shuh)
*Mazurian lakes
Neisse (NY-shu) **River**
Nowa Huta (NOH-vuh HOO-tuh)
Oder (OH-dur) **River**
*Pomeranian lakes
Poznan (PAWS-neyen)
Slask (SHLAWSK)
Sopot (SAW-pawt)
Stare Miasto (STAH-ruh MEE-AHST-vaw)
Szczecin (sh-CHEHCH-een)
Tatry (TAH-tree)
Vistula [Polish is Wista (VEES-wuh)] **River**
Wadowice (vah-du-VEE-tsuh)
Warsaw [Polish is Warszawa (wahr-SHAH-vuh)]
Wawel (VAH-vehl)
Wieliczka (vee-ehl-EETCH-kuh)
Wielkopolska (vee-ehl-kaw-PAWL-skuh)
Wroclaw (VRAW-tswahf)
Zakopane (zah-kuh-PAH nee)
Zelazowa Wola (zheh-lah-ZAW-vuh VAW-lah)

Glossary

barszcz (bahrshch)—beet soup

Cepelia (tseh-PEH-lee-uh)—folk art stores run by the government

Cold War—a period of history, beginning after World War II and ending in the mid-1980s, when distrust grew between Eastern Communist countries and Western powers

czarnina (chahr-NEE -nuh)—fruit soup made with duck and prunes

gorale (goo-RAH-leh)—mountaineers

"Gosc w domu, Bog w domu" (GAHSHCH v DAH-moo, BUK v DAH-moo)—"A guest in the house is God in the house." A Polish saying on hospitality

Hejnal (HAY-nahw)—a trumpet call played every day in Krakow since the thirteenth century

"Jeszce Polska nie zginela, poki my zyjemy" (YEHS- shuh POHL-sku NYE zhu-NYEH-wuh, POO-kee MIH YEH-mih-zhi)—"Poland will never die so long as we are alive"

kapusniak (kah-POOSH-nyahk)—sauerkraut soup

kawiarnie (kah-vee-AHR-nyuh)—coffee houses

kulig (KOO-lihk)—a type of winter party that goes from house to house, gathering more partygoers with each stop

lody (LAW-dih)—ice cream

matura (mah-TOO-ruh)—college entrance exam

mazurek (mah-ZOO-rehk)—a small cake; also a Polish dance

naleszniki (nah- ehsh-NEE-kee)—thin pancakes stuffed with different fillings

nie ma (NYEH MAH)—"no more"

nie pozwalam (NYEH phz-VAH- lahm)—"I disapprove," the words of the liberum veto

obiad (AW-byahd)—biggest meal of the day

oplatek (aw-PWAH-tehk)—a Christmas wafer

paczki (PAWNSH-kee)—doughnuts

pierogi (pyeh-RAW-gee)—dough stuffed with meat, sauerkraut, cabbage, potatoes and cheese, or fruits

pisanki (pee-SAHN-kee)—Easter eggs

placek (PLAH-tsehk)—a kind of small cake

pole (PAW-leh)—field

Polonia (paw-LOH- nyuh)—a Polish-American community

Polska (PAWL-skuh)—Poland's name in Polish

polskie sercy (PAWL- skyuh- SEHR-tsih)—"Polish hearts"

Po Polsku (paw PAWL- skoo)—"in Polish"

przepraszam (pzheh-PRAW- shahm)—"excuse me"

Sejm (SAYM)—Poland's parliament

siekierki (shyuh-KEE-EHR-kee)—long-stemmed hatchets used by the gorale

smacznego (smahch-NAY-gaw)—"enjoy your meal"

smigus dyngus (SHMEE -guhs DING-gus); often pronounced to rhyme, (SHMING-gus DING-gus)—Polish custom where, on Easter Monday, boys and men spray water or perfume on the girls and women they know

Sobotka (saw-but-kuh)—Saint John's Eve, also called Swietojanki

Solidarnosc (saw-lee-DAHR-nohsh)—Solidarity, Poland's first independent trade union, now a political party

"Sto lat, sto lat, niech zyje, zyje nam" (STAW laht, STAW laht, nyehk ZHEE-yuh, ZHEE -yuh NAHM)—"May you live for a hundred years." Words to a song sung to honor people

Sylvester—New Year's Eve

Swietojanki (shvyehn-taw-YAHN-kuh)—Saint John's Eve, also called Sobotka

szczesliwy, szczesliwa (sh-chensh-LEE-vih, sh-chensh-LEE-va)—happy

szopka (SHAWP-kuh)—portable puppet theaters used to act out the Christmas story

wigilia (vee-GEE lee-uh)—Christmas Eve dinner

woda sodowa (VAW-duh saw-DAW-vuh)—soda

wycinanki (vih- tsih-NAHN-kee)—paper cutouts

zloty (ZWAW-tih)—the basic unit of Polish money

Selected Bibliography

Borrell, John. "The Man Who Did His Duty." *Time*, October 1, 1990, 63.

Kelly, Eric P. and Kostich, Dragos D. *The Land and People of Poland*. New York: Lippincott, 1972.

Madison, Arnold. *Polish Greats*. New York: David McKay, 1980.

Mills, Lois. *So Young a Queen*. New York: Lothrop, Lee, & Shepard, 1961.

Popescu, Julian. *Let's Visit Poland*. London: Burke Publishing, 1979.

Sachs, Jeffrey and Janine R. Wedel. "The Economist Heard Round the World: Poland's Great Experiment (Part I and II)." *World Monitor*, October 1990, 30-32, 33-42.

Comic books of Polish legends, coloring books, and other hard to find books on Poland are available through:

    The Kosciusko Foundation Bookservice
    15 East 65th Street
    New York, New York 10021

For more information on books published in Poland in English, write to:

    Interpress Publishers
    ul. Bagatela nr. 12
    00-585 Warszawa POLSKA
    Warsaw, Poland

Index

About the Author

Christine Pfeiffer has had a lifelong interest in international affairs. She has lived in Poland and Germany and speaks several languages, including Polish, German, and French.

Eastern Europe, says the author, is a part of the world unfamiliar to most Americans. "Yet millions of Americans are of Polish descent," she writes, "and Poles have made important contributions not only to the United States but to the world. There is much more to Poland than headlines about political developments could ever imply. It is my hope that young people who read this book will gain insight into Poland's uniqueness—and also into the Poles as people, whose customs are distinct but whose feelings, interests, pastimes, and daily lives have much in common with those of American young people and adults."

An experienced educational writer, the author has written a newsletter for the Polish American Educators' Association of Chicago as well as reading materials for young people and a series of articles for educational magazines. She is a board member of the Polish Arts Club of Chicago. Ms. Pfeiffer has a B.S. and a M.S. from Northwestern University's Medill School of Journalism and resides in Chicago.